MAKE YOUR OWN
BABY FURNITURE

MAKE YOUR OWN BABY FURNITURE

by

FLORENCE ADAMS

M. Evans and Company, Inc.
New York

This book is dedicated to all mothers,
and is intended to offer them a variation on the theme.

Library of Congress Cataloging in Publication Data

Adams, Florence.
  Make your own baby furniture.

  Includes index.
  1. Children's furniture. 2. Wooden toy making.
3. Woodwork—Amateur's manuals. I. Title.
TT197.5.C5A22   684.1'04   80-10495
ISBN 0-87131-320-0

M. Evans and Company, Inc.
216 East 49 Street
New York, New York 10017

Design by RFS Graphic Design, Inc.

Manufactured in the United States of America

9 8 7 6 5 4 3 2 1

CONTENTS

ACKNOWLEDGMENTS

This book was a four-month assignment. I discovered that as I began to write, hoping to build each project as it was designed, the complete task became impossible. Thus, I forfeited the phase I love best, the building, and farmed projects out to friends, doing only a few myself. In the end, this process turned out to be better, for it helped catch all the assumed information that I had left out, as well as provide corrections and suggestions for improvements. And because some of the builders were totally inexperienced, it gave me a measure of whether a project was or wasn't easy . . . how it related to my original estimate . . . and where the hang-ups were . . . what techniques needed more explanation . . . that sort of thing.

Certainly, then, these friends have enhanced the book with their participation, but more to the point, I simply would not have finished in time without their help.

Perhaps it would be helpful for you to know of some of their experiences with these projects.

Diane Brenner, a close friend, spent weekends at my house churning out project after project. She is divorced, with a teen-ager and a pre-teenager. Before coming to play with my tools, as she tells it, her house maintenance did not go beyond hammering nails (whatever size she had available) into plaster walls and living with the concave emptiness that remained after the surrounding plaster cracked off. She watched me, early on, build the first project, the crib, and asked if she could try one. "An easy one, huh?" Sure, I said, and handed her the plans for the changing table. "Oh, this looks terrible!" she said. No, I told her, it's really just a lot of sawing and measuring, then slap it all together . . . bang-bang. Try it! And she did. Deep within me I had an ulterior motive. I felt it was an easy project, but I had to know. She would be the best test. It took her two days. Yes, it was a lot of sawing, she agreed, and early on the first day she came to tell me that she had broken three saw blades already. "What am I doing wrong?" Probably pushing too fast, too hard, which causes the metal blade to heat up and practically melt enough to crack. Go slower, be patient, let the saw work for you. It worked. No more broken blades. Later she asked me how she would have known this. "I guess you wouldn't have without some more experience and someone explaining it. I'd better put some techniques in the book, a special section." She agreed. And so, that chapter grew every time she had a problem.

Diane was the only totally inexperienced builder who contributed. Thanks to her, I do believe, the book is more comprehensive for such a builder. And as it turned out, each time I said a job was easy or more difficult, it turned out that when she finished, she usually agreed.

For her, she says, the experience was mind-blowing. Last week she went out and bought a saw and a drill. "I'm going to renovate my kitchen, build both of the boys desks like the crib . . . and I might even repair all the plaster holes!"

Thank you, Diane.

Barbara Vogel has dabbled for years. She is an intensely involved builder, thinking out, drawing, and redrawing each project before she tackles it, when a functional task is mandatory. Her bookshelves blend into the mood of the room when she's finished, molding and all. (As opposed to mine, which are usually just shelves slapped up.) However, an artist at heart, she is far happier with a scavenged piece of beautiful wood that she is painfully carving and sanding into a spoon or a bowl. As the pressure to finish built, I went to her for help. "Could you bang together some of these projects for me?" I showed her the two tables, the mommy rocker, and the playpen. "This table . . . mortise and tenon joints . . . these are hard for the novice. They have to fit just right. I don't even know if I can do it right." I didn't believe her at first. "Of course you can," I said. But, of course, I knew that my way of tackling that kind of joint would be to do it, and if it didn't fit, was too loose, I'd fit with glue and wood slivers, dab and patch in my way. This would never be the way she did things. "Give it a try and I'll include your experiences. It will help the book."

I'd only given Barbara Vogel scratchy plans for the mommy rocker. "I'm not sure this will work, whether the seat is too big for thighs, if the thing will rock safely. Do you mind trying it to see?" "Sure," she agreed, and she ended up redesigning it. And I'm sure she enjoyed that project the most.

Thank you, Barbara Vogel.

Barbara ended up farming out one of the tables to a friend, Maggie Houghton, who had just started some carpentry classes. Yes, Maggie ended up doing the trestle table and enjoyed the new challenge of the mortise and tenon joints. "They're not easy," she reminded me.

Thank you, Maggie Houghton.

Marge Sinnott is an occupational therapist. She had taken carpentry courses and other structural courses for her work, which included making molded casts for disabled people. Her interest was with the toys, which she suggested we donate to some of the institutions she worked at. And it was she who carved and sanded away at the little people. "There should be more females," we agreed. We were both tired of all the fire*men,* farmers, police*men,* and the like, stereotyping all these toys. "And besides," she added, "it's mostly women who drive the school buses, anyhow."

Marge had the patience I did not, for the cutting and sanding of the blocks, and she had a baby to give the gadget box to. "They can always use more puzzles at the center," she added and she was off. "Please be sure to tell your readers that the toys, above all, must be meticulously sanded, so there's not a chance of splinters."

Thank you, Marge.

Dana Pelligrini is a master carpenter, the finest and most dedicated carpenter I know. I have bowls and planters she has created from three kinds of contrasting wood that, besides serving their "function," offer something magnificent to touch of a moment. And touch and feel and touch. Wonderful! She lives in California right now, and our letters went back and forth feverishly. "What do you call this piece of hardware?" . . . "What kind of joint will work easily?" . . . "What should I use for a covering?" . . . "What kind of paint, varnish, etc.?" She knew it all. She was my reference text.

Thank you, Dana.

Donna Woodward is a hustle-bustle type. She often works three jobs in the summer so she can continue school all winter. She has done almost everything, it seems, loves to try new things, do new things, travel new places. And, in attitude, she is the most like me. Bang-bang, slap-slap, get it done. And because she probably knows more than I do, she gets it done better than I do.

Donna borrowed an ice cream truck and hustled the wood from the store to the various households involved. She hustled together meals (she's the best cook in the crowd and loves doing it!) when we'd all get together for a Saturday night supper and rap about the projects. She helped reassemble the early projects that had been tucked away to make room for the later ones. She picked up our pieces in the final crunch days and made us laugh.

Thank you, Donna.

My two sons also got into the act. David, who is fifteen, is an accomplished builder and the designer of the umpteen tree houses, street vehicles, hockey nets, etc. He is always gathering the gang together for some new project. "David," I said to him, as time was running out, "I need your help. How about the rockers and vehicles?" "OK," he agreed, and after school and homework and on weekends, he plowed away. "We could give them to the new baby next door," he suggested, and we did.

Sam is twelve. He has little interest in building, but that's probably partially because David does it all, even things for him, so he doesn't have to. (Second-child syndrome.) He's the reader in the family. And, I guess, the thinker. Thus, his pleasure lies in research. My greatest anguish was my inability to draw and create the animals and other shapes for the toys. Sam volunteered the search for samples. He traced pages and pages from his children's books, dictionaries, encyclopedias, magazines. "Here, mom, these should give you some ideas," he said one day, handing me the pile of papers. He had heard me moaning and moaning and simply went off on his own to the task and presented me with salvation. My head popped with variations, though many turned out to be impossible to render. However, the end result was that my biggest problem was solved by Sam's quiet, giant contribution.

Thank you, Sam.

I must also say thank you to Jan Roby, Julie Crowley, Marjorie Bernstein, Tracy O'Kates and Betty Scrivani for their suggestions, help, and constant encouragement.

Lastly and firstly, thanks to my Mom, who, though she still has trouble with my "unladylike" carpentry and plumbing skills, concedes that this book is an interesting (proper, I think she means) offering of my talents. Thank you Mom, I'll get you liberated yet.

PREFACE

My introduction to building came from need, and my approach today still reflects that experience. Years ago I bought an inexpensive brownstone that wanted attention in the way of renovation. I could only (barely) afford the cost of materials, but not labor, and decided to try to bumble through it myself. I asked many questions—it seemed everyone in the neighborhood was involved in some phase of renovation—and I began with the smallest and simplest of projects. My primary requirement of the result was that it function—and, as soon as possible. Quality was second to this. Essentially this means that I used methods of construction that were easy for me, a novice, to handle. Nails where I thought they would hold, screws when I thought they wouldn't—which implies that some things nailed had to be screwed eventually because my initial choice was wrong. And I didn't glue much in those days. Sanding and fine finishing were also not important then. Usually I hammered or screwed the corners together and stained or painted the project in an attempt to complete it in one day.

My selection of the final design of a project usually came only after days and sometimes weeks of searching through magazines and books until I found a design that could be accomplished with my early skills and the basic tools I had. Often, if not always, I made modifications that simplified it more; for example, I always butt-jointed the corners. (Butt joints are corners that meet end to edge, flush, as opposed to lap or dovetail joints, which required more tools, experience, skill, and time than I had. Today I still opt for butt joints, and am still satisfied with the results.

However, I do use glue more often, and sand and finish more frequently. (My biggest dose of this was with the projects for this book, which mandated more care from me because they were for babies who need protection from rough and splintery wood.)

Early on I was taught the principles of predrilling before screwing, and of careful, straight, slow sawing. This is half the battle. My compulsive nature caused me always to double- and triple-check my measurements. This is terribly important and I recommend such compulsiveness as a habit, particularly when you are the designer. When such was the case for me, I graphed the project three dimensionally on 10-squares-to-the-inch graph paper so that I could carefully check the sizes of wood involved.

Another thing I did—chalk it up to my methodical Virgo rising—was to keep all my tools hanging on a wall for easy access. I arranged my hardware, nails, screws, etc., on shelves by size and type: screws separated from common nails separated from finishing nails, etc. This setup allowed me to check immediately to determine if I had what I needed or if I had to shop. When I get a bug in my bonnet to make something, I want to do it yesterday and once started, I can't stand it if I have to stop and run to the store—or can't get to the store if it's Sunday.

We are all different in our approach. My choice of preliminary organization allows me a security when I begin the actual work. And my resolution comes, basically, from the recognition of my psyche, that I will be totally wiped out if I can't bang the whole thing together in an afternoon. "Slap-bang" is often how I refer to my approach, or rather, technique. A simplified design, basic tools I can handle, and a speedy finish.

Now I must admit that as a beginner I turned out many a wobbly and tilted bookcase that I wedged into shape between two pieces of furniture, but for me that was acceptable. Today, fifteen years later, I have begun to try more difficult projects and have even given thought to designing a project that would blend in with the room it is to live in, adding edging or hiding cleats—that sort of thing. Perhaps it is because the pressure of renovation is off; perhaps it is because my experience bolsters me, gives me the added security to dare more; and perhaps with age, a patience is coming to me. But not so totally that I have given up my quest for an "easy" project.

For example, for six months I have been researching solar greenhouses because the time has come when I "must" have one. I went through every book, pamphlet, and magazine on the market, or so it seems, and finally made a design decision that felt fairly settled within me. It was, however, a tricky design that I knew I'd have trouble with, and it would be expensive. A few days ago I visited a friend who is a builder and we talked about the project. He listened and finally said, "Why don't you use . . . and build it . . . and on and on . . ." I didn't even know about the product he suggested, which costs 10 percent of what I'd been planning to use. And because of the product (corregated fiberglass) my design became simple, and I am excited to begin. Motto: talk it up, ask questions, find people with experience and learn from them; but also, be unafraid to try your own methods, for surely these lessons will be your best growing experience. And be happy with your own stopping place.

PARENT TO PARENT

As I remember it now, it seems that during the three months before my first child was born, I spent endless hours looking for material to make curtains . . . happy, fun, baby-kind curtains. Then, when I found it, I languished away many more hours sewing them by hand. What else did I do? Yes, little origami fish, all colors, to hang on mobiles. And . . . I waited. Being home was new to me. I had been working for ten years since finishing school. What does one do all day long? (I had my answer after baby-birthing started.)

How differently I see things now. Some years later, after my divorce, I found myself boldly renovating my brownstone, learning not to be afraid to handle tools or fumble through tasks I once thought impossible, just to save a buck. Well, in the beginning it wasn't exactly "quality," but it was functional. And in any case, I had graduated from the "Contact Paper Queen of the neighborhood"!

When I moved from New York City to Cape Cod four years ago, there was more to do. Bookcases . . . children's rooms . . . tree swings . . . and the recycling of some wonderful dump pickings. Summer yard sales yielded old furniture to be restored. And now, though this may not be a total blessing, I buy nothing I can build. At times I feel smug, but there are other times when I am impatient for something we need and curse my damnable economic smugness. In the end, I save much money, feel a measure of pride, and I have fun.

So here I sit, looking back on those dull three months before David was born, and fantasize. Oh, the things I could have made for my new baby! Instead of those blasted origami fish, I could have built him a world! Furniture that would recycle with him as he grew older. A changing table that could become shelves for his fuzzy animals, or just a bureau. A high chair that would detach into a table and chair for the animal tea parties. I remember the gadget box that hung on the side of the playpen. I could make one of those. Sure. With doors that open and close. A color twirl. A noisemaker. Why not? In fact, I could make the playpen! And the fantasy goes on. . . .

This offering, then, is my fantasy. You may get caught up in it. If you do, you may think it is a present for your baby, but it isn't. It's a present for yourself!

The environment you design for your child's life with you, from birth until she leaves home, is more important than you can imagine. As important as the atmosphere of her loved ones is the personal world she lives in, as a baby, a toddler, a small child with her own wonderful fantasies. It is not so much the amount of space as what is in it . . . the wallpaper, the bed, the toys . . . these are her very special things. Her joy, her peace, her growth are as much wrapped up in these as they are dependent on your love.

So if you build and plan with love—and a keen and calculating eye to the future—you may be able to give her a more special world.

I hasten to add, though it will spoil the mushy mood, that if you give your child peace, she will give you peace! Yeah! I suppose my most favorite cliché during those early years of mommying was "a happy mommy is a happy baby." This I believe. (There have been some rough times for me and the boys, times when mom wasn't so happy, and it evidenced itself in their happiness and moods.) Anyway, what this sometimes cynical old mom is saying is, give a mind to yourself when you give to the kid.

There are some other things you should think about as you plan for your baby's new world. How long is a baby a baby? How many babies do you plan to have? What if you have twins? (Forget that. If that happens, all the questions and plans start over.)

Take the crib, for example. A crib is probably the most expensive piece of furniture bought for the baby, generally costing well over a hundred dollars these days. And after a few years it's obsolete. What a waste. If you are planning a short and quick breed of two, then for five or so years you could use a sturdy crib and then convert it to a couch or a youth bed or even a desk. Of course, if you're planning a big family, let the crib be a crib be a crib be a crib . . . and then firewood.

Me, I bought the conventional heavy-duty crib that withstood two quick boys and then gave it away. Scrounged old doors for desk tops when they grew up. But the desks could have been born with them, if I'd been into building them then. I'm sure you will see possibilities I haven't thought of. Go to it.

About me, I am still a "functional" builder. This means two things: one, I build what I need and rarely have enough time to do the "magnificent" job; two, I am not a "fine carpenter." I have, therefore, evolved this slap-slap, bang-bang approach. My constructions are sturdy all right, but I require designs that guarantee easy projects, projects that fit within the limits of my tool collection and within the boundaries of my experience and daring. I do not, for example, have a router or a radial arm saw . . . just a bunch of hand-held electric tools.

So, what I'm trying to say is that the designs included here are tailored for the small tool supply, to be accomplished by a fairly inexperienced builder. Many of the designs offer versatility, a future life when the child is no longer a baby. The furniture isn't dead-ended after three or six months.

This book doesn't stop at the last page. Rather, it starts there. Whether you know it or not, as soon as you begin to construct some of the projects in here, you will begin to see hundreds of other things you may want to try. You'll open the Sunday newspaper sale supplements and see a toy you are sure you could make. You can. It will start happening. Better still, you may even improvise on my designs—and I'd be the first to admit some of them could be spruced up. (I'm certainly not the creative designer I'd like to be. I live with my "functional" characteristics and more often than not see wonderful, clever, and simple projects that I wish I'd thought of. But I didn't.) When you're done being worn out by mommying and things begin to flow smoothly, there will be things for yourself or dad or a friend that you will want to build. Some things you might want to build later are truly difficult to construct without far more elegant tools than I suggest here. You might even consider a fine carpentry course. Excellent! But there are many things that do not pose much of a problem.

Get into the habit of looking at how things are made. Adapt what you see to the tools, space, money, and skills you have available. You will be surprised at the new world you entered when you began to build your baby's world. After all, it's also yours.

Finally, be happy in your work. I am happy, truly, when I decide on a project and doggedly finish it in a day—a very long day sometimes, when I send the boys off to fend for themselves, cook the meal, that sort of thing. (This action naturally requires a reciprocal amount of patience from me when they are up putting walls on the third story of their fourth tree house and are not ready to come to dinner yet.) Yes, be happy. If you are a new builder, play with some scrap lumber for a week or so. Try the saw, the drill. Hammer some nails. Try working out some of the suggested techniques in a later chapter. Then you'll be ready to start.

Almost everything we built was finished in one or two days. Try the cradle for a starter. It's one of the first things you'll need and it will give you cheer when it's finished—and hope, and a marvelous sense of accomplishment. Or try anything else that looks to you like a good starting place.

Being practical, I also suggest that you remember that you will also curse and spit sawdust, wishing to be finished, at times. This, too, is part of it. But as the pieces begin to fit together, you will be happy. At least I wish for you what is true for me.

Let this book and its offerings take you and your baby where it will.

Tools/Supplies

Your tool collection is your most important asset, whether or not you are an experienced builder. Tools are simply an extension of your arm and serve to multiply your strength manyfold. A hammer, for example, offers a weighted head meant to aim at a nail and drive it in. The power of your arm's thrust and the heavy hammer head center to a small area to energize the hammering. An electric drill will bore a hole faster and easier than a manual drill.

Being a lazy and impatient builder, I do not wish a project to take forever, nor do I want it to wear me out too early. For this reason I use electric hand-held tools. There are some who believe you have more control with manual tools, but I have not found this to be true for me. Let them have their control, if it's true. No way do I want to hand-saw a piece of plywood for thirty minutes with a hand saw when I can do it in five or ten minutes with an electric saw.

There are other supplies you will need—nails, screws, and glue, for example—and here I recommend the economic approach. Buy large boxes, not small plastic-bagged packages. Now is the time to consider stocking up on these necessities. Glue should be bought in a large container, too. Use carpenter's glue, not just plain white glue. It will hold better. (My choice is Elmer's Carpenter's Glue.)

You will also need things like nuts and bolts and washers for some projects. These you should buy, as "loosies," as you need them. A good hardware store usually has open bins for nuts and bolts, cheaper this way than packaged. By the way, find out now where the best hardware store is, not a "housewares store." Buy from such a place rather than a supermarket or mall store, where the quality might be inferior.

On the subject of quality—don't chintz on tools either. Ask around and buy a good or medium-to-good, recommended brand. Some manufacturers produce different levels of quality depending on price.

When it comes to electric tools, look for double-insulated encased tools. These will save you the trouble of three-prong adapters and grounding. However, if you do use electric tools with three-prong plugs, it is mandatory that you be grounded. This means plugging the tool into a three-prong outlet. (The third prong, the round one, is the ground. If the motor breaks in such a way as to allow the electricity to reach the casing, this third prong is connected to a wire attached to the casing inside and will deliver the dangerously loose electricity out through its wire to the "ground," eliminating a shock to you.) However, if you do not have three-prong outlets, use an adapter that allows you to plug your device with three prongs in one side. The other side has two prongs for the wall and a small wire with a curved piece of metal at the end. Unscrew the wall socket plate a bit and slip this wire metal end under and screw tight again. The plate screw screws into the box in the wall, which should be grounded. Thus, the little wire acts like the third-round prong. *Please, always be sure you are grounded.*

If you are going to buy an electric saw, buy one that allows you to adjust the sawing angle, so that you may saw angles other than only 90°.

You will also be using hinges. There are butt hinges and offset hinges. These types are illustrated later.

Cotter pins, often used with dowels, are neat. They slip through a small hole, stopped by a large head at one end. The ends on the other side spread open to provide a secure hold. Cover them with cloth tape, and check them frequently for loosening.

Angle irons offer a squared corner added security, while flat irons can further secure flush joints.

Half-round braces will hold dowels in place while giving them freedom to turn.

Back to nuts and bolts and washers for a minute. Because I hate to turn the screwdriver so much, I always defer to nuts and bolts whenever I can reach both surfaces of two pieces of wood being joined. Just drill a hole and slip the bolt through. Washers should always be used at both ends to keep the bolt head and nut from sinking into the wood as it is tightened. For a more permanent hold, lock washers should be used. They are like washers, only sliced open and made rigid in a slightly offset-open way. They act like a spring between the nut and the wood (or a regular washer between wood and lock washer) and keep the nut from loosening.

MAKE YOUR OWN BABY FURNITURE

TOOLS

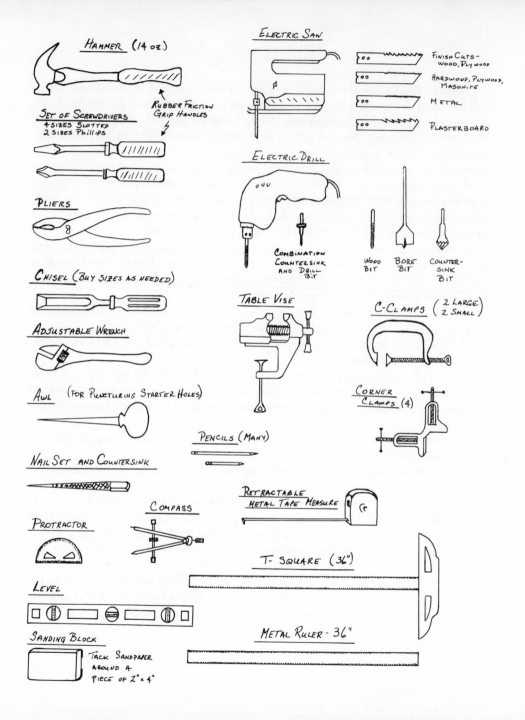

HAMMER (14 oz.)

RUBBER FRICTION GRIP HANDLES

SET OF SCREWDRIVERS
4 SIZES SLOTTED
2 SIZES PHILLIPS

PLIERS

CHISEL (BUY SIZES AS NEEDED)

ADJUSTABLE WRENCH

AWL (FOR PUNCTURING STARTER HOLES)

NAIL SET AND COUNTERSINK

PROTRACTOR

LEVEL

SANDING BLOCK
TACK SANDPAPER AROUND A PIECE OF 2" x 4"

ELECTRIC SAW
FINISH CUTS— WOOD, PLYWOOD
HARDWOOD, PLYWOOD, MASONITE
METAL
PLASTERBOARD

ELECTRIC DRILL

COMBINATION COUNTERSINK AND DRILL BIT

WOOD BIT

BORE BIT

COUNTERSINK BIT

TABLE VISE

C-CLAMPS (2 LARGE 2 SMALL)

CORNER CLAMPS (4)

PENCILS (MANY)

COMPASS

RETRACTABLE METAL TAPE MEASURE

T-SQUARE (36")

METAL RULER- 36"

WOOD SCREWS (FH = FLATHEAD ⌲)

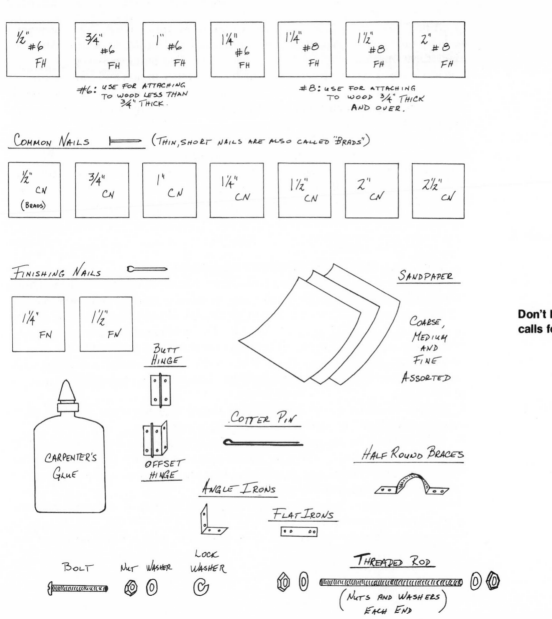

| ½" #6 FH | ¾" #6 FH | 1" #6 FH | 1¼" #6 FH | 1¼" #8 FH | 1½" #8 FH | 2" #8 FH |

#6: USE FOR ATTACHING
TO WOOD LESS THAN
¾" THICK.

#8: USE FOR ATTACHING
TO WOOD ¾" THICK
AND OVER.

COMMON NAILS ⊨———→ (THIN, SHORT NAILS ARE ALSO CALLED "BRADS")

| ½" CN (BRADS) | ¾" CN | 1" CN | 1¼" CN | 1½" CN | 2" CN | 2½" CN |

SUPPLIES

FINISHING NAILS ⊏———

| 1¼" FN | 1½" FN |

BUTT HINGE

OFFSET HINGE

CARPENTER'S GLUE

COTTER PIN

ANGLE IRONS

FLAT IRONS

SANDPAPER

COARSE,
MEDIUM
AND
FINE

ASSORTED

HALF ROUND BRACES

BOLT NUT WASHER LOCK WASHER

THREADED ROD

(NUTS AND WASHERS
EACH END)

**Don't buy all at once, but as each project
calls for what you don't have yet.**

A final suggestion, from one who is admittedly opinionated. Don't keep your tools in a toolbox. Forsake that digging through and fitting back in frustration. Hang them up somewhere. A wall, a closet door. And build shelves for your nail and screw boxes. Keep leftover nuts and bolts together in jars and cans by size, on the shelves, too. If you have an old box of assorted nails, screws, etc. that you've been scratching through every so often, put it away for the ultimate emergency and start afresh.

The biggest asset of this type of organization is the time you will save trying to discover if you have enough of the supplies or not.

Finally, buy a big garbage can and throw all your small scrap wood ends into it. Sooner or later you'll surely be looking for a small scrap. And it makes excellent kindling for a wood stove or fireplace.

CONSTRUCTION TECHNIQUES

PREDRILL BEFORE SCREWING AND NAILING

The entry of a screw or nail into wood causes some wood displacement. Often there can be enough displacement to cause the wood to splinter and crack, rendering the wood useless. Thus, it is important to predrill holes for the screw, getting rid of just enough wood to avoid cracking. The hole should be small enough so that there is still enough wood left to accept the threads of the screw. (If it goes in too easily, the hole is too big!) The drill bit should be a mite smaller than the solid center of the screw at about midway down. There are two easy ways to make a choice of bit.

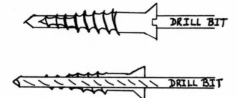

DRILL BIT

DRILL BIT

1. Hold a bit and a screw between your thumb and forefinger and roll them together. You should be able to feel if the size is right.

2. Hold the drill bit behind the screw up to the light. With the screw held in front, you should only be able to see the bit behind it near the point of the screw. With the drill bit in front, you should be able to see the threads of the screw and a tiny edge of the solid center of the screw.

It seems to be a generally accepted practice to prepare the hole in three stages, involving three different drill bits.

1. Countersinking for the flathead to be flush with or below the surface of the wood.

2. A larger hole for the initial entry.

3. A smaller hole for the second piece of wood, where the holding must happen.

By countersinking the screw below the surface of the wood, you can later cover the space with wood putty, sand, and paint or stain and make the screw hole almost invisible.

Three changes of drill bits for one hole! Yuk! I must admit that I've always skipped one of these steps and just countersunk after drilling one hole through, a tight hole, which always makes me feel secure . . . thus a tougher job.

However, a friend has finally enlightened me to a wonderful gadget—a three-in-one combination drill bit. Imagine! Countersink, first hole, and second, graded, all in one. Better still, they are available for different size screws! No guessing and hoping. No thumbing. I buy one as I need it for a particular size screw, and keep it in the box of screws.

So, here's my advice. Though they're expensive, use these three-in-one bits; at least get the #6 and #8 for 1¼″ screws. Those are the ones you will use most often.

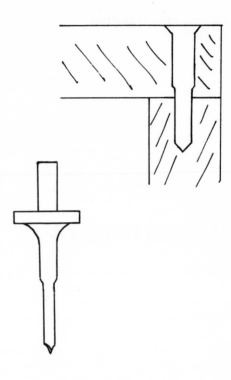

CUTTING OUT SHAPES

In order to cut out a shape within a piece of wood, first predrill a hole along the *inside* edge of the shape line, using a drill bit slightly larger than the width of the saw blade. Then you can slip the saw blade in and cut the shape out.

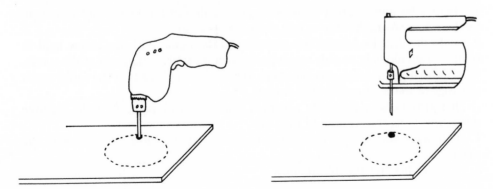

DRAWING THE LINES FOR SAWING

Use your T square to draw the lines on the wood along which you will cut. Press the back wedge of the T square flush to the edge of the wood to assure a perpendicular line.

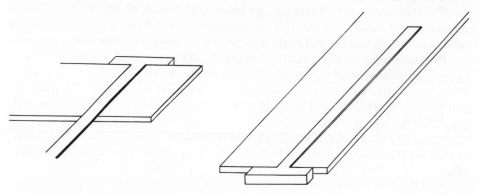

MEASURING AND SAWING

After measuring and drawing a line for a saw cut, remember that the pencil line indicates the length. Rather than cutting through the line, cut to the side of it, yielding the true length after the cut.

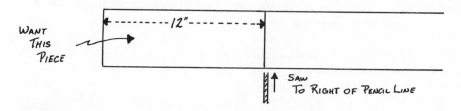

A saw blade has a thickness that is lost from the thickness of the wood after the sawing.

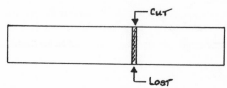

Therefore, I make the following recommendations. Measure for only one cut at a time. In the sample below, if you premeasure for the five cuts all at once and then cut, through the center, say, you will lose the thickness of the blade, which might be 1/32″ or so.

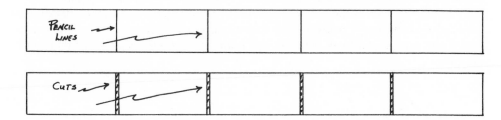

This is also true when laying out the measurements on plywood. Even though the illustrations show the whole panel with the cuts all laid out, don't measure for all of them at once. Do them one at a time, cut, then measure for the next. Or, for a group of pieces the same size, you can cut across the panel.

The next illustration demonstrates how you should take some care first and decide where your first cut will be.

Saw horses are a must when dealing with plywood. (See appendix for how to build them.)

This could be a tough one for a novice. Where to start? 4′ x 8′ panels are unwieldy and should be cut in half (or thereabouts) first. However, if I premeasure for pieces 1, 2, 3, and 4, and then cut along the lower edge of 4, I will later lose the thickness between 4 and 1, 2, and 3, since the saw blade is thicker than the pencil line.

So, it will have to be that the first cut is made after measuring for 1, 2, and 3. (And cut right through to the other side of the panel.) Then move the panel along the sawhorses, measure for piece 4, and cut it out, again going to the other side of the panel.

Now you can go on, or go back and measure for 1, cut it out, measure for 2, cut it out, cut off the excess edge, cut the excess off 4, etc.

Note: Work toward leftover areas, don't start at them.

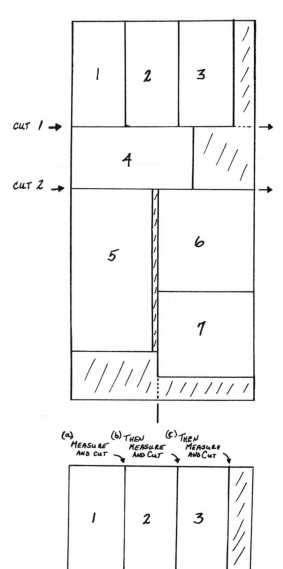

ABOUT PLYWOOD

Many of the projects in this book call for plywood. Plywood today replaces the very wide boards that were available to the early settlers, who had access to ancient and gigantic trees. Rarely, now, can you get boards wider than 11½″.

Plywood is manufactured by gluing an odd number of thin panels together. Each panel is made of a number of wide, thin boards, to bring the panel size to 4′ x 8′. An odd number of these 4′ x 8′ panels are glued together, the grain direction alternating, from panel to panel, top to bottom, left to right, as they are placed and glued. The procedure of using an odd number of panels keeps the panel from warping.

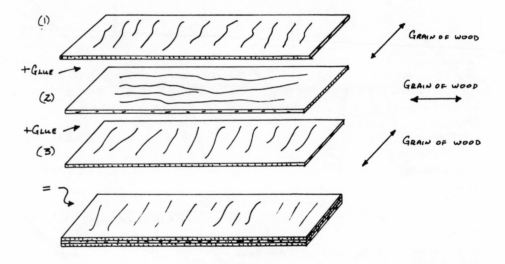

Plywood comes in various thicknesses. It is available in "interior," "exterior," and "marine" quality. Exterior and marine types have been glued together with waterproof glue. Marine quality is the longest lasting outdoors and the most expensive. If you built something for outdoors with interior plywood, after a while the thin panels will begin to separate as the glue is washed away by rain.

Plywood is also available in various grades. It is graded by the quality of the two outer surfaces. When both surfaces are very good—no knotholes or splits, nice and smooth—the grading is A-A. One less good side would be A-B. The most common, and the cheapest, is A-D—one very good side, one bad side, marred with knotholes and splits, but just as structurally sound as A-A. Thus, wherever your projects will need only one good side showing, use A-D. (The knotholes and splits can be filled with wood putty and sanded.)

SAWING THROUGH PLYWOOD

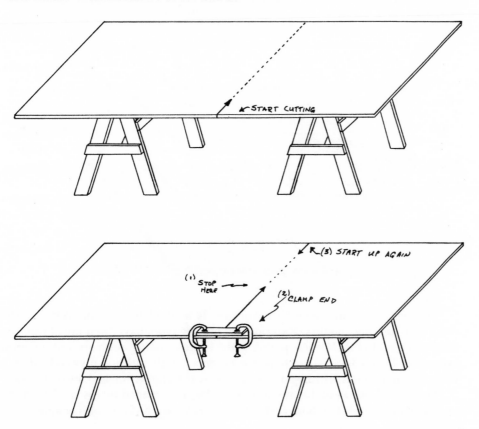

4' x 8' plywood panels are heavy and difficult to maneuver. You really should use sawhorses to lay them on for sawing, as opposed to using two chairs for narrow boards.

Because they are so heavy, if you cut straight through from one end to the other, the two sections will topple, falling inward or outward.

If you have a friend helping, she could hold the already cut end to prevent this, but if you are alone you should stop sawing about half the way and clamp a thin piece of wood to the cut ends. (You don't want to do this too soon after starting because it could constrict the saw blade; halfway through is a good stopping place. (Besides, you can't reach much farther.)

Then go around to the other side and start sawing from the end of the line inward to meet the end of the first cut.

SQUARING BOXES

About the best way to hold perpendicular pieces of wood together while pre-drilling and screwing is with corner clamps. They not only hold the pieces together—usually an impossible task for the solitary builder—but they square the corners at 90°. (How often before I discovered these clamps did I end up with a lopsided box, thinking mistakenly that I had eyeballed it together OK!)

However, it is often difficult to work with all four clamps functioning at once, particularly if you are nailing and ought to have the opposite end of the wood against a wall or something so it won't slide from the hammering.

STABLE SURFACE

No!

The screw ends of the clamps protrude, which would mar the wall.

In these cases I just put two clamps on, do my work at one end, then switch the clamps to the other side and work there.

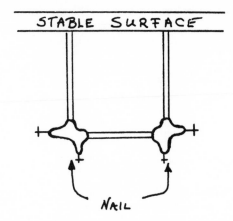

Next, the whole box, half-done, must be carefully turned over onto one side, then the next, so it's upside down. Now these corners can be clamped and screwed together. Or you could hammer a thin nail halfway into each corner before you turn the box over, to hold it together.

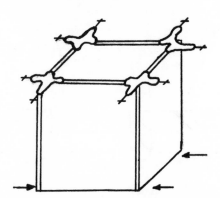

MAKE YOUR OWN BABY FURNITURE

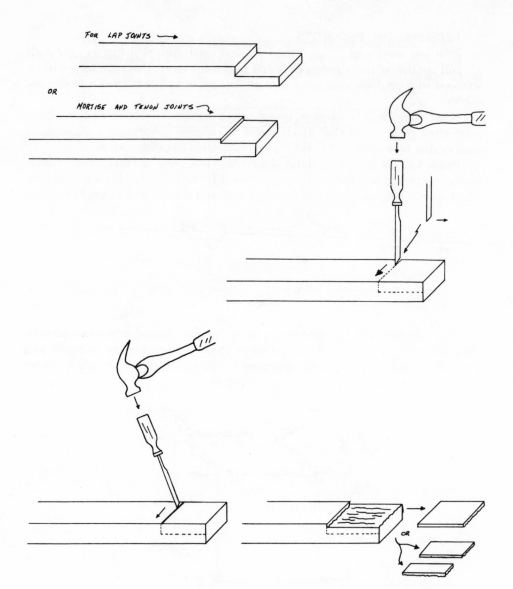

FOR LAP JOINTS →

OR

MORTISE AND TENON JOINTS →

NOTCHING OFF 2" x 4" ENDS

1) Measure for the piece to be removed and draw lines to guide.

2) Place the chisel along the line (bevel toward the edge), and hammer it in a way all along the line.

3) Tilt the chisel and hammer again, and it should cause a thin layer to come off—move the chisel under as you hammer. The layer may come off in two pieces if wide.

4) Go back and repeat steps 2 and 3 until you have removed the desired depth.
A bit of gentle chiseling will smooth the craggy layer top remaining, and then sanding will finish it.

OR

FINISHING THE PROJECTS

First you must sand . . . and sand . . . and sand. Rub your fingers over it all . . . pull out the splinters and go back and sand some more. Use a sandpaper block wrapped with medium sandpaper to start, fine paper to finish. Or use an electric sander.

Some things will be painted. Be sure to buy nontoxic, lead-free paint. Spray paint often gives a smoother finish, but if you choose to spray, be sure to use a good quality face mask and stand the recommended distance away.

Painted or not, the outer finish should be a few coats of vinyl spray or polyurethene, sanding rough spots between coats. This will be a durable seal of plastic which should hold up under the expected wear and tear even of a hungry teether.

USING THIS BOOK

Each project is introduced by some opinionated propaganda. (I guess that's what you call it.) This is followed by a step-by-step descriptive procedure. The illustrations that follow are arranged in the sequence of work to be done. In the back of the book you will find a shopping list for the materials for each project.

In the illustrations, you will notice that I define board wood by its "name" and by its actual dimensions. For example: 1″ x 6″ (¾″ x 5½″). Board lengths are "named" to their closest inch size, but in actuality are usually ½″ thinner in thickness and approximately ½″ narrower in width. Thus, they are called: "one by four," or "one by ten," etc. After "1 x 1," "1 x 2" and "1 x 3," board lengths are only available in even number inch widths: "1 x 4," "1 x 6" . . . . . . "1 x 10," which means, in actual size: (¾″ x 3½″), (¾″ x 5½″) . . . . (¾″ x 9½″). Throughout the book I have referenced both the name of the board and the actual dimensions, so that the measured layouts are clear.

The first pages of these illustrations, *Materials,* show what wood and hardware will be required and also the cutting diagrams for the wood. Rather than repeat this in each step-by-step procedure, let me discuss, here, how to accomplish the plywood cuts. Measure for only one cut of 48″ across the board at a time and then cut. As I have mentioned, the saw eats up a fraction of the wood as it cuts and you want your cuts to be as precise as possible. Put the section aside and measure for and cut the next 48″ cut across the board. When these larger cuts are finished, go back and cut the smaller pieces from each section, for then you'll have more space in the room after the board has been diminished. I have marked suggested "first cut, second cut," etc. on the cutting diagrams of the plywood as a guide. As much as you'd like to sit down and measure out the whole piece of plywood ahead of time—*don't!* The same rule applies to lengths of wood. Measure for and cut one piece at a time.

The illustrations also show how the pieces fit together. Look, for example, at the changing table drawer (illustration, p. 67). See the dotted lines at the ends of the back, with the arrows from the sides going into the space between the ends and the dotted lines. This means that the sides go *between* the back and front, the edges of the sides meeting the face of the back and front.

Where patterns are required, get yourself some large graph paper and paste or tape enough pieces together to make the paper the same size as the project. Draw dark lines for the inch representation. Move your finger along the book diagram, inch by inch, and put a dot or x every actual inch on your large graph. Then connect the dots and cut the pattern out and trace it onto the wood.

I suppose the thing that hung me up the most was the angle cuts. Be cool . . . and careful . . . and take what you get, which will probably be fine. (That's what I did. On paper you will see that I state an angle of 80° in addition to the lengths, for example. God knows what angle I got myself, but it worked fine.)

A last-minute suggestion. The desk portion of the crib (page 79) may well be the most satisfying and fun project to start with. Try it and then use it as your worktable. If you're like me, you may sometimes need an inspiration—a kind of mushy feeling of accomplishment, and a sense of showing-off pride. This could provide it.

Whenever you feel uncomfortable about a technique, practice on a piece of scrap first. And don't be afraid of mistakes. I made a few grandiose ones with some of these projects—the high chair came out doll-size! (Back to the drafting table!)

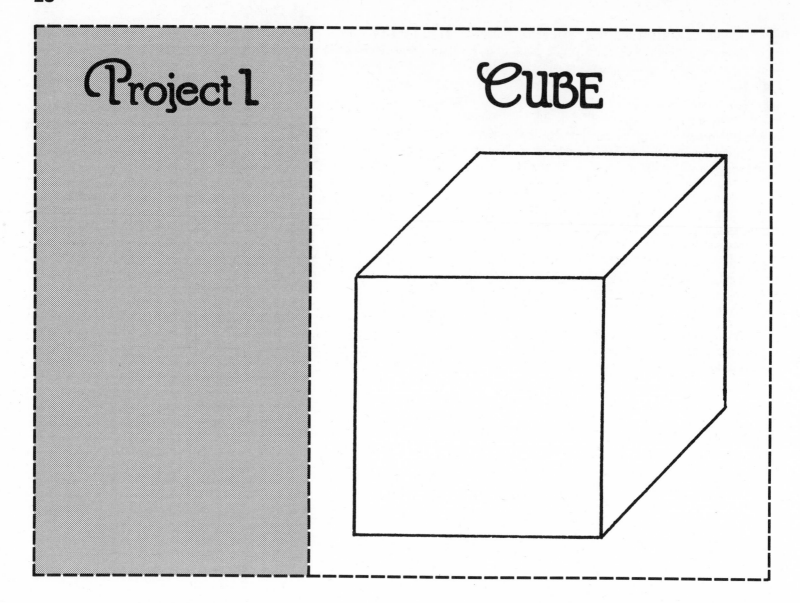

Project 1

CUBE

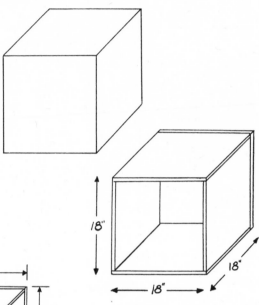

or anyone who has never done much building before, the construction of a cube will serve as a most useful lesson. (And the cube itself will be a most versatile product of the lesson, as I will illustrate later.)

A cube is a box that is the same size on all sides. For the sake of this demonstration, we will consider the *outside* dimensions as those which are equal.

First, it is not enough to draw a shape called a cube in an outline manner, as shown. Rather, it is necessary to make the illustration one which will be clear enough to show the most important ingredient in terms of measuring: the thickness of the wood and how the pieces join together.

Looking carefully at this second drawing, you will see that I have illustrated that the top and bottom will be outside, with the sides between them. It will be an open cube with only a back, no front. The back will be attached to all four edges: the top, bottom, and sides. The cube will be 18″ x 18″ x 18″, made of ½″-thick plywood.

Note: Throughout the book, notice how the pieces are joined and how this relates to the dimensions of the projects.

Now, let's take another look at the cube.

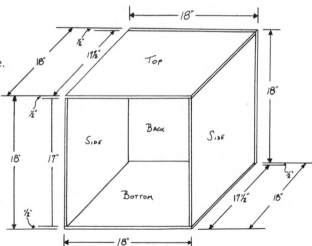

Because the plywood is ½″ thick, and because of the placement of the top and bottom to the sides, the five pieces of wood are not the same size. The *back* is 18″ x 18″. The *sides* are each 17″ x 17½″. The *top* and *bottom* are each 18″ x 17½″.

The sizes of wood are therefore dependent on the design of attachment.

Once I decided to make a cube and cut five pieces 18″ x 18″. Although I got the sides, top and bottom together, it was not exactly cube. However, the back was then too small. As you can see from the drawing, the back should have been 18″ x 19″. So, I just nailed it onto the two sides and lived with it, but that's how I am.

You are the designer and can decide your type of attachment. Often, if you are making a bookcase, for example, you would like a smooth surface on top, as the cube offers, as opposed to how it would look if the top were between the sides and thus had edges at both ends. Further, if you will be using the top to put more books on, there will better support if the top is sitting on the edges of the sides rather than between them.

There is an alternate design to the cube attachment, if you prefer to use the same size wood all around. Four pieces of ½″ plywood, 18″ x 18″ will assemble like this:

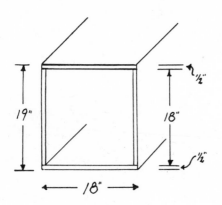

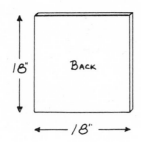

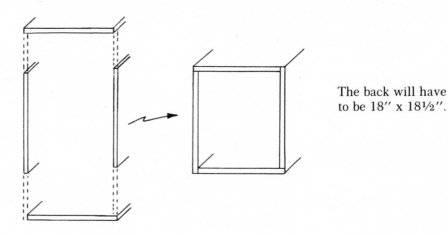

The back will have to be 18″ x 18½″.

The cube may be any size you wish, and you can vary the lengths of wood to create rectangles instead. The laying out of your plans will be the same. If you draw your plans on graph paper, ten squares to the inch, you will be able to check your measurements easily.

Depending on what work will be required of the cube, you can either glue and nail the pieces together, or glue and screw the pieces together for firmer support. The box may have a tendency to wobble left or right, but once the back is affixed, the unit will be squared.

And what can you do with a cube . . . or cubes . . .?

ROLLING STORAGE
FOR UNDER SHELVES
OR BEDS

OR

TOYBOX ON WHEELS

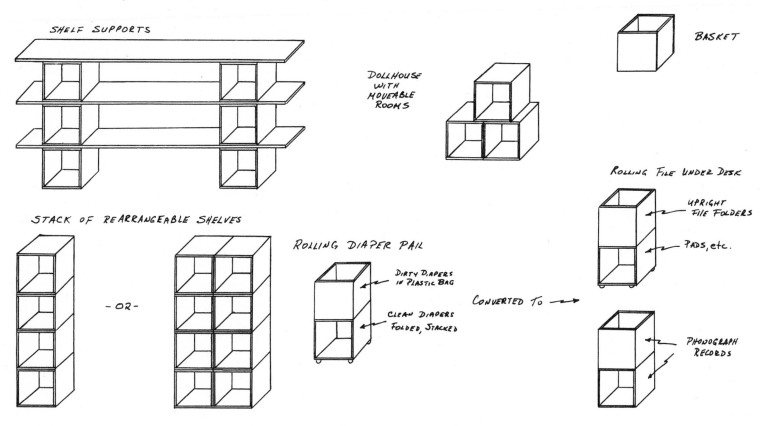

SHELF SUPPORTS

DOLLHOUSE
WITH
MOVEABLE
ROOMS

BASKET

STACK OF REARRANGEABLE SHELVES

-OR-

ROLLING DIAPER PAIL

DIRTY DIAPERS
IN PLASTIC BAG

CLEAN DIAPERS
FOLDED, STACKED

CONVERTED TO →

ROLLING FILE UNDER DESK

UPRIGHT
FILE FOLDERS

PADS, etc.

PHONOGRAPH
RECORDS

Project 2 CRADLE/TOYBOX/ROCKING CHAIR/SHAKER CRADLE

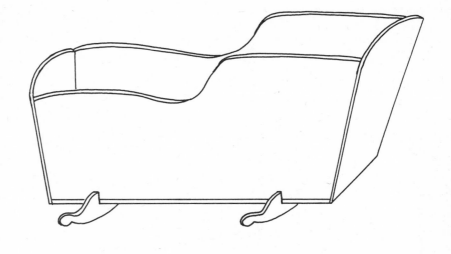

My sister lent me her cradle. It was the typical style, like a miniature crib, with fancy carved bars all around, and it was suspended at the ends so it could be rocked. I put it right beside my bed—first mistake—so I could be near my brand-new baby . . . most handy for that syndrome that sets in immediately after arriving home from the hospital with the first baby: leaning way over to listen for the breathing . . . every ten minutes or so.

Those first few weeks are so crazy, so fraught with sleeplessness, so complicated by the mixed emotions of wanting to sleep (how do you pretend to be asleep to an infant?) and trying to get with the scene of new mommy and new baby. I only remember that my daytime was a juggle. I didn't use the cradle. I used the carriage. I nursed him and tossed him back into the carriage and dived onto the couch to grab a few minutes' sleep. But I kept my foot on the handle of the carriage and pushed it back and forth with each renewed whimper. Sometimes we both slept. Sometimes I said over and over to myself, "Babies are supposed to cry, relax!" And he cried and I slept. Or, naturally, there were times when he went right off and I lay there wide-awake, though bleary-eyed, unable to sleep.

I remember mostly about that time right after my first son was born, that I simply was not prepared for the scene. No one told me I might get angry at this tiny cherub. No one told me that I would get no sleep. No one suggested that I bottle feed so my husband could share the middle-of-the-night trudge.

And then comes the first night he sleeps through the night . . . how you wake and run to him, thinking him dead . . . but there he is, sound asleep. Suddenly it has happened. You are free. And maybe you cry a little from the surprise, from the release, forgetting, or simply unaware of, what's to come next. I was thirty-one when I had my first child and it seems that I didn't know a damn thing about what to expect.

If I were to start all over, I would wish for the invention of a cradle that rocked by sound—sound of baby-crying would throw a switch to start the rocker motor. I would dial in the times of feeding. Better still, I'd install a similar rocker under me. Then we could both wake slowly, getting rocked, and I'd bring him into bed with me for his feeding and be rocked at the same time so he wouldn't wake up too much.

So I guess what I'm really saying is, maybe you'll be prepared and maybe you won't. Don't hassle it. Don't feel guilty.

Now, about the cradle. It's a matter of choice. You may want one. Or you may, like me, use the carriage. A nice box or drawer is actually good enough, for you only use a cradle for a month or three, if I remember correctly.

You want a cradle. OK. How about a rocking cradle that can later be transformed into a toybox and a rocking chair? This is what I include here. Also included is a Shaker-style cradle, for those who might prefer a traditional type. Later it, too, could convert to a toybox . . . or a planter . . . or anything you might imagine.

CRADLE—PROCEDURE

1. Measure for the first 48″ cut on the plywood and cut. Measure for the second cut, and cut. Measure for the third cut, and cut. (Notice from the diagram that the third cut is not straight across the 48″.)

2. From these sections cut out the smaller pieces, sides, and square pieces for the ends.

3. Measure for the 1″–0″ diagonal cuts that will taper the sides and ends, and cut off the sections; start cutting at the 1″ end.

4. Make an actual-size pattern for the rocker ends from the design included and trace it onto the plywood section. Cut out rocker ends. Use a scroll saw blade for this cutting. A scroll blade is not as wide as other blades and will turn the curves easier.

5. Sand all sections, over and over, until smooth and safe.

6. While working on the rocker ends, measure for and draw the lines for the future placement of the rocking chair seat and back.

7. Perhaps a friend could help with this. Glue the edges of the ends. Place the ends between the sides and hammer in thin finishing nails at the upper and lower corners to hold the unit together. Later you can countersink them (drive them beneath surface) with a hammer and nail set, and fill the holes with wood putty.

8. At the end of each side, about ⅜″ from edge, measure down 1″ and mark for a screw at each corner and one centered between them.

CRADLE/TOYBOX/ROCKING CHAIR

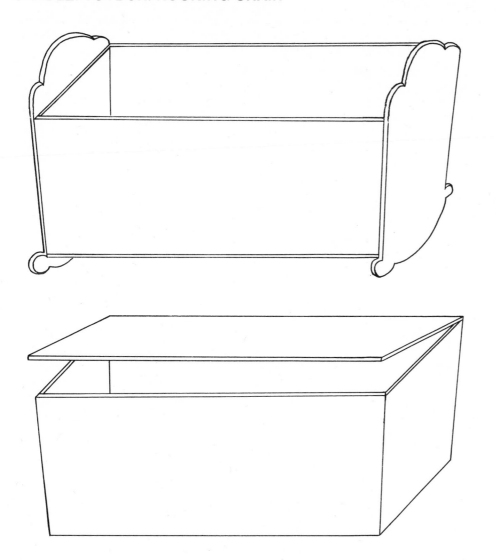

9. Use a combination countersink drill bit and predrill for the twelve screws. Then screw the screws in.

10. Turn the unit upside down, glue the edges, and lay the bottom on. Measure, in a similar manner to the sides measurement, for the 12 screws. Sit on the box—this makes a great clamp—and predrill for the screws. Then screw in the screws. Use 1¼″ #8 flathead screws for this whole unit.

11. See the cradle end worksheet diagram; measure 2″ in from sides and 1″ up and down from where top and bottom of cradle box will meet rocker ends, and mark for screws.

12. Stand the cradle unit on one end, lay the rocker end in position on top. Use large C-clamps to hold the rocker end to the unit and predrill for the screws. Screw in the first rocker end. Stand the unit on the opposite end and repeat the process.

13. Run your hands along all surfaces and do any additional sanding required. Finish according to your choice—paint or stain and cover with a layer or two of clear vinyl spray.

14. Store the toybox lid, rocker seat, and back for the future.

CRADLE/TOYBOX/ ROCKING CHAIR—MATERIALS

¾" plywood (A-D).

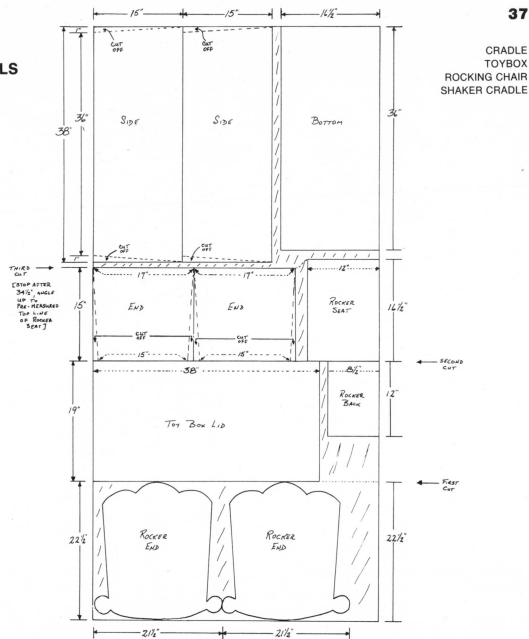

CRADLE
TOYBOX
ROCKING CHAIR
SHAKER CRADLE

MAKE YOUR OWN BABY FURNITURE

**CRADLE ROCKER END—
WORKSHEET (1)**

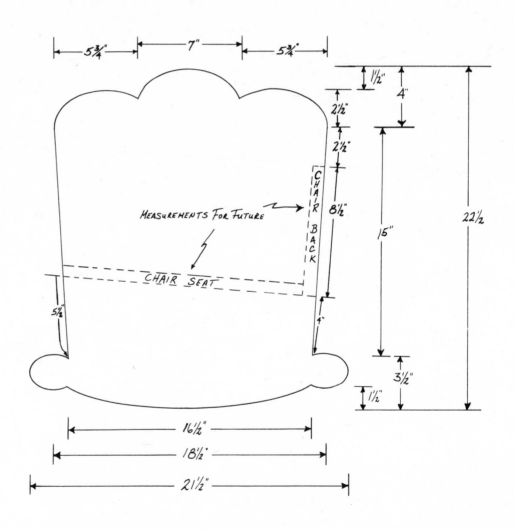

**See next pages for measuring detail and
templates.**

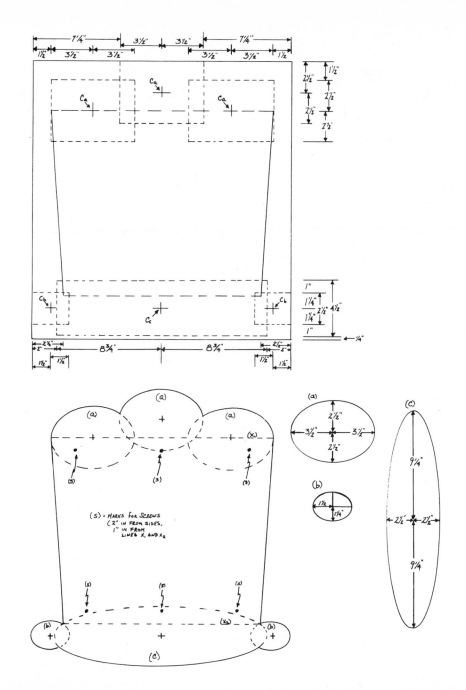

CRADLE
TOYBOX
ROCKING CHAIR
SHAKER CRADLE

CRADLE ROCKER END— WORKSHEET (2)

Ca = center A ellipse.
Cb = center B ellipse.
Cc = center C ellipse.

See Appendix for How to Draw Ovals of Any Size.

(S) = MARKS FOR SCREWS
(2" IN FROM SIDES,
1" IN FROM
LINES X₁ AND X₂

See next page for templates for (a), (b), and (c).

CRADLE ROCKER END

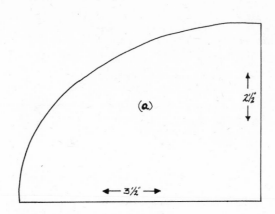

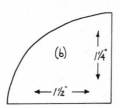

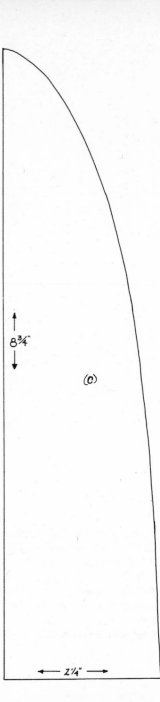

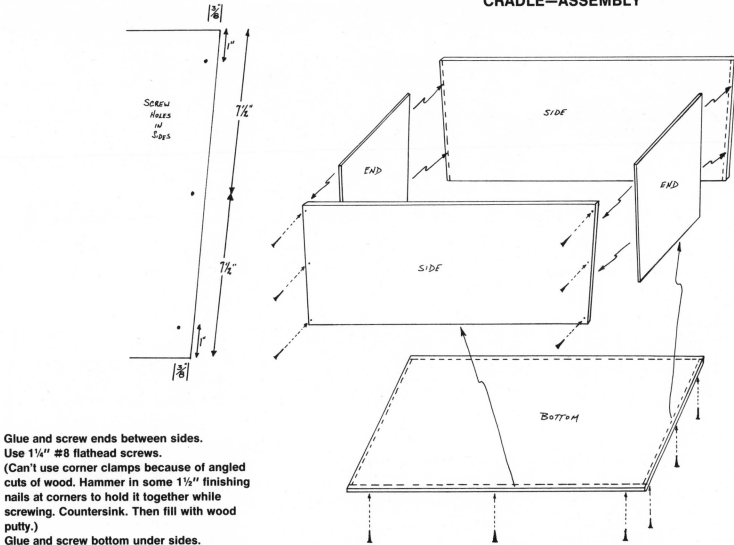

SCREW HOLES IN SIDES

3/8"

1"

7½"

7½"

1"

3/8"

SIDE

END

END

SIDE

BOTTOM

Glue and screw ends between sides.
Use 1¼″ #8 flathead screws.
(Can't use corner clamps because of angled
cuts of wood. Hammer in some 1½″ finishing
nails at corners to hold it together while
screwing. Countersink. Then fill with wood
putty.)
Glue and screw bottom under sides.

CRADLE/TOYBOX/ROCKING CHAIR—ASSEMBLY

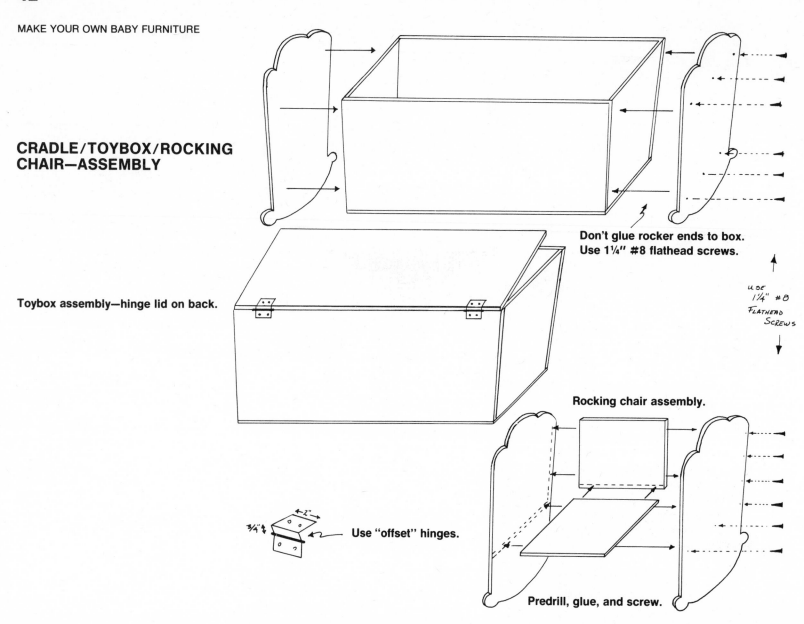

Don't glue rocker ends to box. Use 1¼" #8 flathead screws.

use 1¼" #8 FLATHEAD Screws

Toybox assembly—hinge lid on back.

Rocking chair assembly.

Use "offset" hinges.

Predrill, glue, and screw.

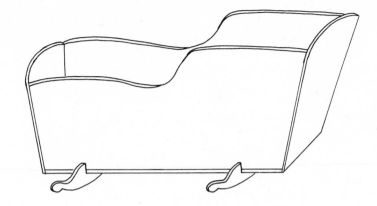

SHAKER CRADLE

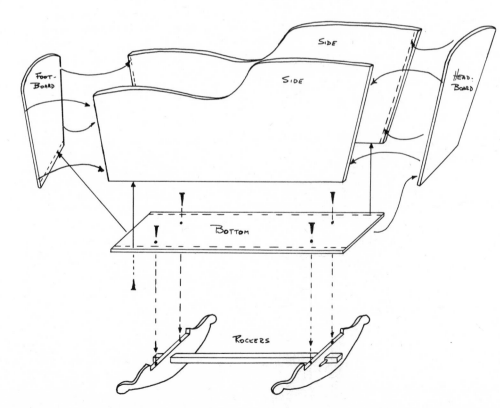

Headboard and footboard screwed *between* sides.

Bottom *under* sides; *between* headboard and footboard.

Rockers joined by pegging brace screwed into bottom.

MAKE YOUR OWN BABY FURNITURE

SHAKER CRADLE—MATERIALS

¾″ plywood (A-D).

See next page for circle segment for top of headboard, footboard, and rocker.

1″ x 6″ (¾″ x 5½″).

1″ x 1″ (or baluster: 1-1/16″ x 1-1/16″).
⅜″-diameter dowel pegs.

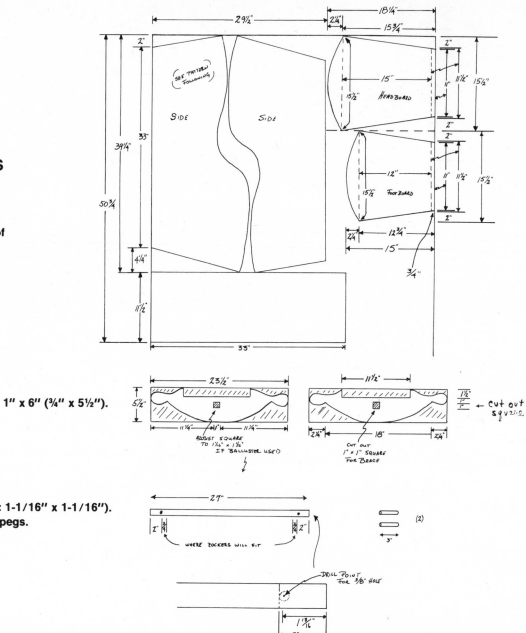

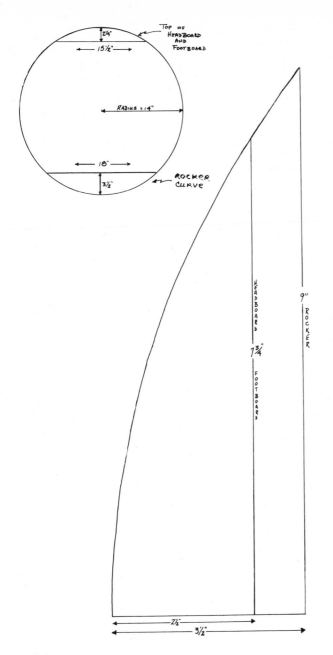

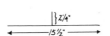

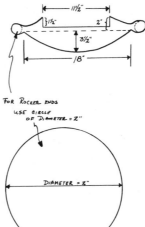

SHAKER CRADLE—
WORKSHEET FOR TEMPLATES
HEADBOARD, FOOTBOARD,
AND ROCKER

In order to derive the circle segment for the top of the headboard and footboard, I fooled around with a compass until I got a segment 2¼" high and 15½" wide. The resulting circle had a radius of 14".

I used the same size circle to give me the rocker curve.

For rocker ends use a circle of 2" diameter.

MAKE YOUR OWN BABY FURNITURE

SHAKER CRADLE—SIDE PATTERN

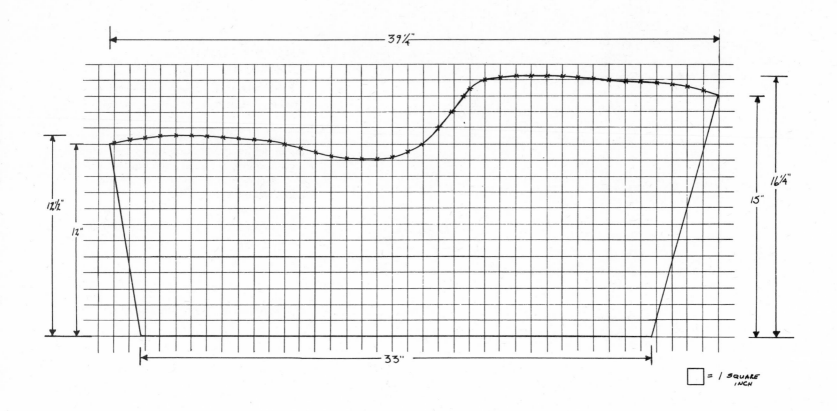

□ = 1 SQUARE INCH

When cutting bottom board, use angle
variation on saw to angle the saw blade so
that edge will meet headboard at 75° (instead
of 90°) and the other edge will meet footboard
at 80°.

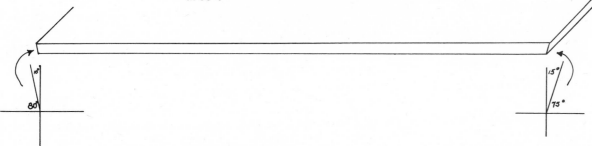

Project 3

CHANGING TABLE/ BUREAU/CABINET

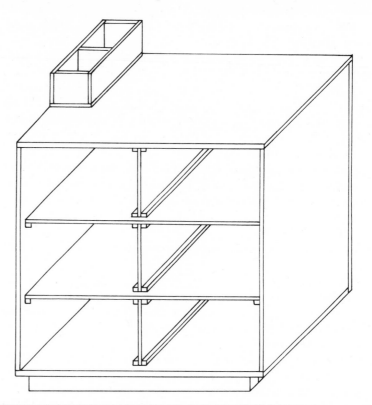

othing should be a waste, which means that anything you build for a small baby should be able to be used for the toddler, or even the teen-ager. Thus, I suggest recyclable furniture, furniture that can grow with the child to serve another useful function.

My husband converted my drafting table into a changing table by adding two shelves underneath for the diapers and clothing. I thought it was fantastic. I still do. If you think so, and want to pick up a drafting table, which adjusts to all heights, do it, and skip this chapter.

The changing table is the place where you must be able to lay the baby down (and strap her in so she doesn't fall off); and you must be able to reach the clean diapers and the dirty-diaper pail, must have some cream handy, a wet facecloth for wiping, and, yes, some clean clothes to replace the wet ones. All this. More: there should be some distraction, such as a mobile, to keep the baby from squirming and whining. Something to keep her from reaching for the pins to put in her mouth. (How about some origami fish??)

My suggestion is an open-shelved cabinet, waist-high, which is a comfortable position for changing. The top can be padded with some thick quilted material covered by a rubber pad—not exposed rubber, but the kind that feels like felt, cotton-covered rubber—that can go into the washing machine. An old belt cut in half and screwed to the ends of the table will make a sufficient strap.

Later on, the changing table becomes a cabinet with doors or a bureau with drawers. No waste.

The plans for the changing table may seem, at first glance, complicated. If you look carefully again, you will notice that I've arranged for slots—for the shelves to sit on—and for the shelf supports to slip through. The slot cleats are all nailed on the individual pieces of wood lying flat on the floor. When the "box" is assembled, everything just slips into place.

The drawers may be added later—if you don't opt for plastic dishpans—and/ or doors. The drawers are simply a box construction of four sides, butt-jointed, with a bottom nailed into the four sides. An extra front piece is added to flush the outside lineup. For a new builder this is an easy drawer and it works well. Later, if you get into this carpentry stuff, you may want to replace them with dovetail-jointed drawers with bottoms inset in routed grooves.

The shelves have been set back an inch for the addition of either drawers or doors. The doors may be inside the box framework or outside, your choice. Doors can be two pieces of plywood cut to fit and hinged to the sides. As you will see from the plans, it will cost more to build six drawers than to hang two doors.

Have fun.

CHANGING TABLE—PROCEDURE
First piece of plywood (see illustration, p. 54)
1. Measure for first 48″ cut, and cut.
    Measure for the second cut, and cut.
    Measure for the third cut, and cut.
    Measure for the smaller cuts from the large sections, and cut them out.

Second piece of plywood (see illustration, p. 54)
2. Measure for the first 48″ cut, and cut.
    Measure for the second cut (54½″ along the 96″ length 10″ from edge), and cut.
    Measure for the third cut, and cut, delivering back and shelf.
    Measure for the shelf supports on the long piece, and cut them.
3. From the length of 2″ x 4″ cut two lengths of 32″ and two lengths of 18½″.
4. From the parting bead cut 16 lengths of 22″. These will become the cleats that hold the shelves and shelf supports in place.
5. Sand all sections, surfaces and edges, over and over until smooth.
6. Following the diagrams, measure for and draw guidelines on the insides of the sides, top, and bottom for the cleat positioning.
7. Nail the cleats onto sides, top and bottom. With the sides placed within the edges of the bottom (see later illustration), stand the three pieces on their front edges (front edges on floor) and glue and corner-clamp the four corners.
8. Measure in from the edge ¼″, then 1″ from each corner, for the screws, then add a centered mark for the middle screw.
9. Predrill for screws, using the countersink drill bit for 1″ screws, and screw in the six screws.
10. Remove top clamps, apply glue to the upper edges of the sides and bottom, and lay the back on the upper edges.

CHANGING TABLE/BUREAU/CABINET

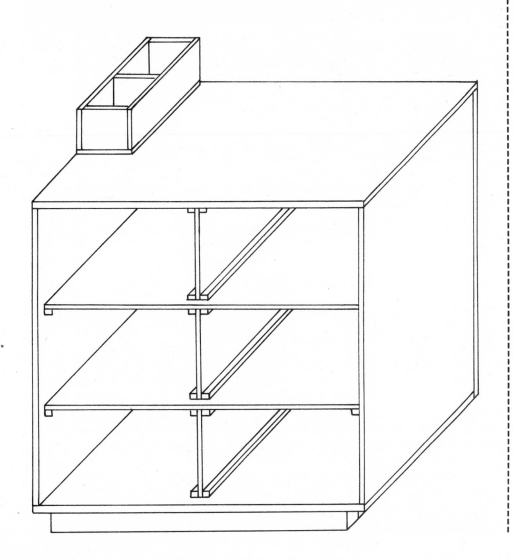

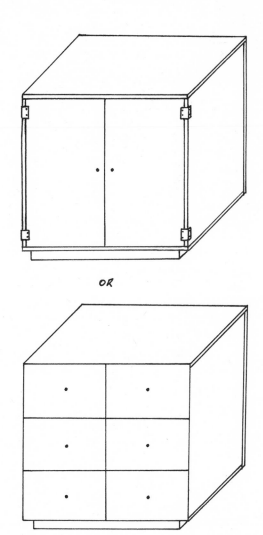

OR

CHANGING TABLE

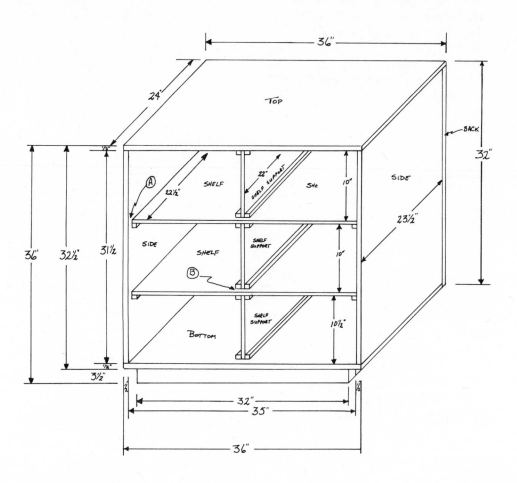

Shelf set back 1″.
Shelf support set back on shelf ½″.

11. Measure for the screws, again, ¼″ from the edge, 1″ from each corner, and two more equally spaced from the end screws.

12. Corner-clamp the back to the open side ends, sit on the back, and predrill for the 1″ #6 flathead screws. Screw in the 16 screws.

13. Keep the corner clamps attached and turn the unit to sit on the bottom. Then remove the clamps. Apply glue to the top edges and lay the top on the edges so that it is flush with the back. There will be an overhang in front.

14. Corner-clamp the top to the open ends of the sides, measure for the screws, predrill, and screw in the screws, attaching top to sides and back.

15. Glue and corner-clamp the base pieces, with the 18½″ pieces of 2″ x 4″ between the 32″ pieces. Nail the corners together, two 2½″ common nails per corner. You may want to clamp only two corners and have the open ends against some support like a wall in order to hammer effectively, or you may use the four clamps and have a friend stand with her feet as a support at one end while you hammer at the other end.

16. Sit the box on top of the base so that the base is flush with the back and 2″ in from each side. The top width of pieces of wood forming the base is 1½″, so measure and mark the inside of the bottom as follows: ¾″ in from back, 2¾″ in from each side and 2″ back from front edge. Hammer 1½″ common nails in at each corner, two spaced between in front and back and one centered on each side (see illustration, p. 59).

17. Sit the shelves on the side cleats and slip the three shelf supports through the shelf, top, and bottom cleats (see illustration, p. 59).

CHANGING TABLE—MATERIALS

½" plywood (A-D).

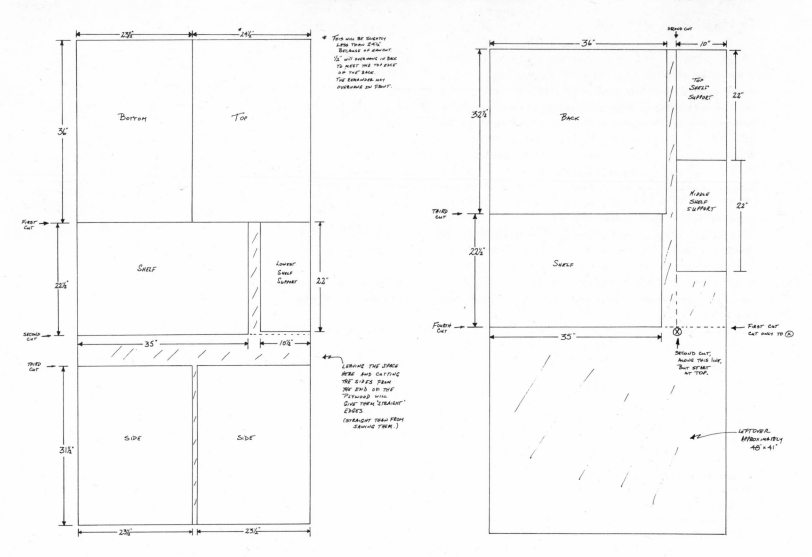

* THIS WILL BE SLIGHTLY LESS THAN 24½" BECAUSE OF SAWCUT. ½" WILL OVERHANG IN BACK TO MEET THE TOP EDGE OF THE BACK. THE REMAINDER MAY OVERHANG IN FRONT.

LEAVING THE SPACE HERE AND CUTTING THE SIDES FROM THE END OF THE PLYWOOD WILL GIVE THEM 'STRAIGHT' EDGES. (STRAIGHTER THAN FROM SAWING THEM.)

SECOND CUT, ALONG THIS LINE, BUT START AT TOP.

FIRST CUT, CUT ONLY TO ⊗.

LEFTOVER APPROXIMATELY 48" × 41".

CHANGING TABLE—MATERIALS

2″ x 4″ (1½″ x 3½″) for base.

32″

(2)

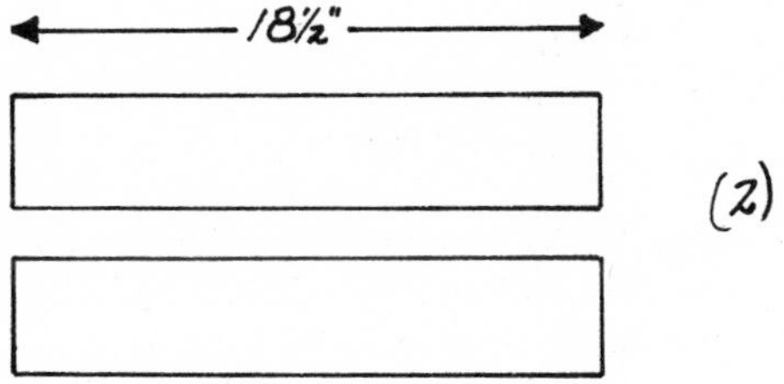

18½″

(2)

Parting bead (⅜″ x ¾″).

(16)

22″

Carpenter's glue.
¾″ brads.
1″ #6 flathead screws.
2½″ common nails.
1½″ common nails.

MAKE YOUR OWN BABY FURNITURE

CHANGING TABLE

Top, bottom, sides, and shelves should be
premeasured for clear placement. Then the
cleats can be glued and nailed on. (Use thin
brads ¾″ long) Mark the insides of sides "top
and bottom" and try to angle the cleat nails
slightly downward, toward "bottom." Mark
insides of top and bottom: "Front" and
"Back."

Top:

Bottom:

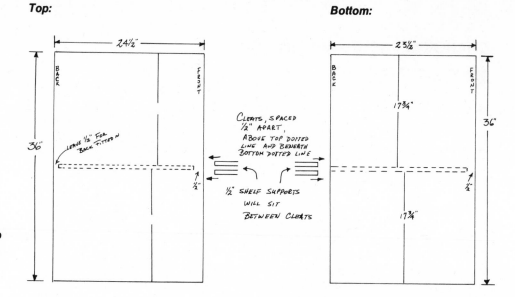

Sides:

Shelves: Measure both surfaces of shelves
(top and underneath). (Cleats will go on both
surfaces.)

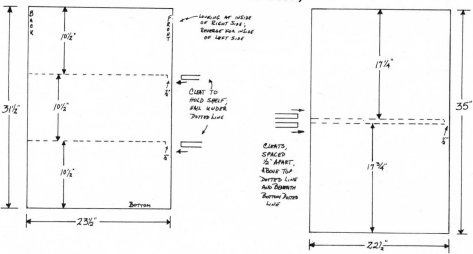

CHANGING TABLE—ASSEMBLY

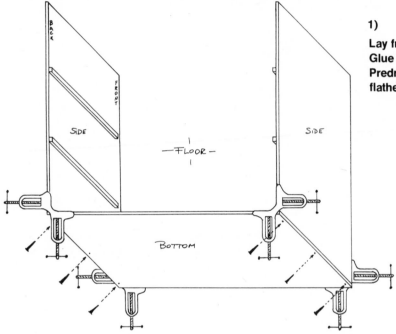

1)

Lay front edges of sides and bottom on floor.
Glue and corner-clamp sides to bottom.
Predrill and screw bottom to sides. Use 1″ #6
flathead screws.

2)

Remove corner clamps. Leaving bottom and
sides as they are, apply glue to back edges
and lay back squarely on top of edges.
Predrill and screw back to sides and bottom,
using 1″ #6 flathead screws.

Note: The top cannot be attached during this
procedure because of the front and back
overhang.

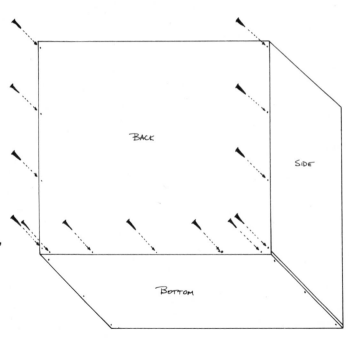

CHANGING TABLE—ASSEMBLY

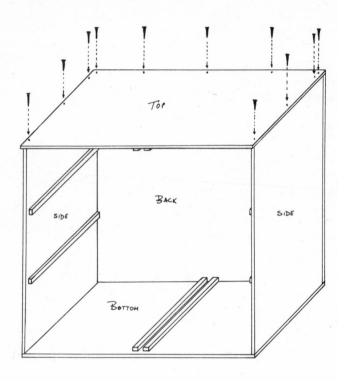

3)

Carefully turn sides and bottom up, with bottom on floor. Glue top edges and lay top on sides and back.

Predrill and screw top into sides and back, using 1″ #6 flathead screws.

4)

Join the four pieces for the base with corner clamps, 18½″ pieces between 32″ pieces. Nail corners together using 2½″ common nails.

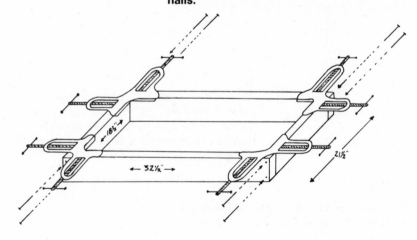

CHANGING TABLE—ASSEMBLY

5)

Glue top edge of base. Lay box on base. Set base 2″ from each side and set back to be flush with back.
Nail bottom of box to base, using 1½″ common nails.

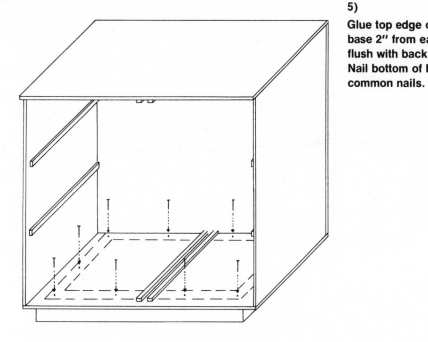

6)

Finally, sit shelves on sides' cleats and slip shelf supports in through cleats of top, shelves, and bottom.

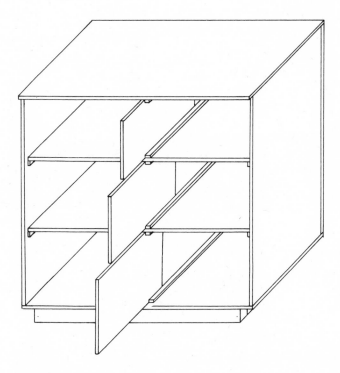

BOX FOR TOP OF CHANGING TABLE—PROCEDURE

A piece of ½″ plywood 15″-plus x 18″-plus will be all that is needed.

1. Premeasure for each piece, one at a time, and cut out the bottom, then sides, then ends and center piece.
2. Glue the unit together, with ends and center between sides, placing the bottom under the edges of sides, ends, and center piece.
3. Use 1″ nails and nail all the sections together.

BOX FOR TOP OF CHANGING TABLE—MATERIALS

½″ plywood (A-D).

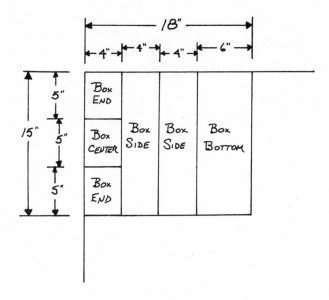

BOX FOR TOP OF CHANGING TABLE

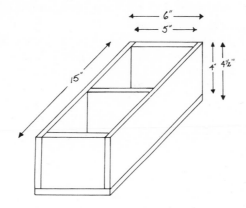

MATERIALS

½″ plywood (A-D).

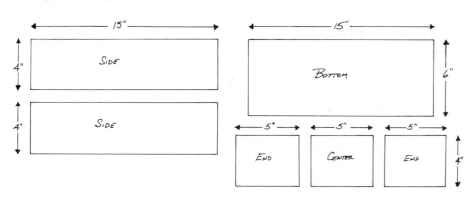

ASSEMBLY

Glue pieces together with carpenter's glue and let sit for a few minutes. Then reinforce by nailing together. Use 1″ brads.

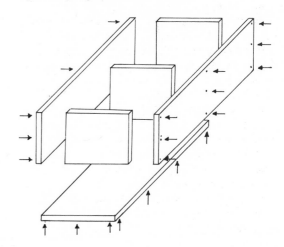

CHANGING TABLE/BUREAU—DRAWERS

Basic box frame:

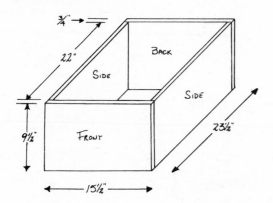

Frame with drawer front added:

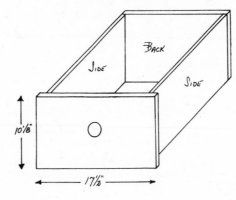

top 2 drawers

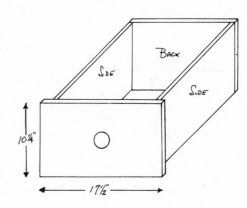

middle 2 drawers

The basic box frame is made for each drawer. Then the drawer front is screwed onto box front. It will be a bit higher and lower and wider than the box front so as to hit the edges of the cabinet and cover the spaces between the drawer sides and the cabinet sides and supports. The box is not as wide as the space it fits into.

The drawer fronts are different sizes. Each is ⅛" lower than the bottom of the box front.

The top drawer front is ½" higher than the box to fit under the cabinet top overhang.

The middle drawer front is ½" + ⅛" (⅝") higher to provide a top overlap.

The bottom drawer front is ½" + ½" + ⅛" (1⅛") higher to provide a top overlap of ⅛" and to cover the extra ½" of shelf space for the bottom shelf.

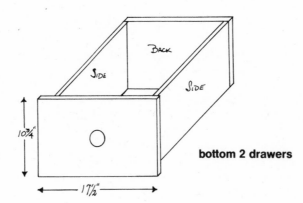

bottom 2 drawers

DRAWERS FOR THE CHANGING TABLE—PROCEDURE

First piece of plywood

1. Measure for the first 48″ cut, and cut it.

Measure for the second cut, and cut it.

Measure for the third cut, and cut it.

Measure for the fourth cut, and cut it.

2. One at a time, measure for the sides from the first and second 22″ sections, and cut them out.

From the two 15½″ sections cut out the fronts and backs.

From the last section measure for the remaining front, back, and sides, and cut out.

Mark each pieces as you cut it and put in separate stacks for sides, tops, bottoms, fronts, etc.

Second piece of plywood

3. Here we are going to break a rule. Measure for all six bottoms at once, and cut *through* the measured lines to get the bottoms. The reason for this exception is that the bottoms will go inside, between sides, front and back, and the slight wood loss will allow it to fit within better. End of exception.

5. Measure for the third cut, and cut it.

6. Measure for the top and middle drawer fronts, and cut one at a time.

7. Measure for the fourth cut, 21½″ in on the 48″ side.

8. Measure 10¾″ in and cut out the first bottom drawer front.

Measure 10¾″ in again and cut out the second bottom drawer front.

Assembly of each drawer (Use 1″ #6 flathead screws.)

9. Glue sides between front and back.

10. Stand drawer box on back, predrill through front into sides, and screw front to sides.

11. Turn over, standing the unit on the front, predrill through the back into sides, and screw back to sides.

12. Set bottom within, but up about ¼″ from all bottom edges of sides, front, and back, gluing it to sides, back, and front.

13. Set it on one side, predrill through other side and screw side to bottom. Then set it on the other side and repeat procedure. Set it on the front and predrill and screw back to bottom. Then repeat with it set on the back, and predrill and screw front to bottom.

14. Mark the six drawer fronts: "top," "middle," and "bottom" on the inside. Measure the inside side of each for proper placement against the front of the drawer box, measuring as shown in diagrams.

15. Turn each drawer front over and on the front side measure for the knob hole, which will be centered, as shown.

16. Glue the drawer front to the front of the drawer box front, using the pre-measured lines as guides and nail with 1" brads.

17. Stand unit on the drawer front. Measure for two spots between the center from the sides, and centered between top and bottom. Nail, from inside, the front of the drawer box to the drawer front (see illustration, p. 67).

18. Stand the unit on the back, predrill for the knob, from the outside in, and slip the knob screw through. Put a washer on, and then the nut, and tighten the nut so the knob is secure. The knob attachment holds the two fronts securely together, the glue and nails help keep the front from tilting out of alignment.

19. Wax all the edges for smooth movement of the drawers.

1" x 10" PINE FOR DRAWER UNITS:

1. Measure for one piece at a time and cut out of lengths of wood.

2. Assemble according to preceding directions, beginning at step number 9. (Use 1¼" #8 flathead screws for pine.)

½" plywood (A-D) or 1" x 10" pine boards (¾" x 9½").

½" plywood (4' x 8').

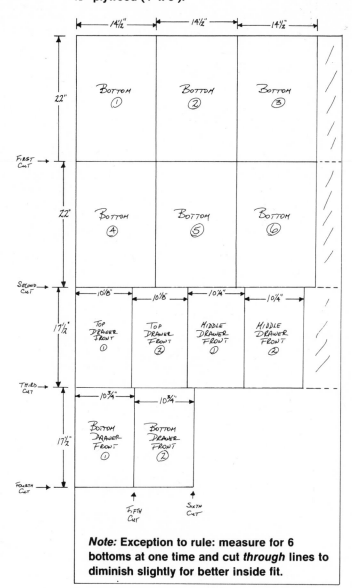

SIDE ①-1	SIDE ①-2	SIDE ②-1	SIDE ②-2	SIDE ③-3

← FIRST CUT

SIDE ③-2	SIDE ④-1	SIDE ④-2	SIDE ⑤-1	SIDE ⑤-2

← SECOND CUT

FRONT ①	BACK ①	FRONT ②	BACK ②	FRONT ③

← THIRD CUT

BACK ③	FRONT ④	BACK ④	FRONT ⑤	BACK ⑤

← FOURTH CUT

FRONT ⑥	BACK ⑥	SIDE ⑥-1	9½"
		SIDE ⑥-2	9½"

22"

Dimensions left column: 22", 22", 15½", 15½", 15½". Top widths: 9½", 9½", 9½", 9½", 9½".

Right diagram widths: 14½", 14½", 14½". Left heights: 22", 22", 17½", 17½".

BOTTOM ①	BOTTOM ②	BOTTOM ③

FIRST CUT →

BOTTOM ④	BOTTOM ⑤	BOTTOM ⑥

SECOND CUT →

Widths: 10⅛", 10⅛", 10¼", 10¼"

TOP DRAWER FRONT ①	TOP DRAWER FRONT ②	MIDDLE DRAWER FRONT ①	MIDDLE DRAWER FRONT ②

THIRD CUT →

Widths: 10¾", 10¾"

BOTTOM DRAWER FRONT ①	BOTTOM DRAWER FRONT ②

FOURTH CUT →

FIFTH CUT ↑   SIXTH CUT ↑

Note: Exception to rule: measure for 6 bottoms at one time and cut *through* lines to diminish slightly for better inside fit.

CHANGING TABLE/BUREAU DRAWERS—MATERIALS

Leftover ½″ plywood (A-D).

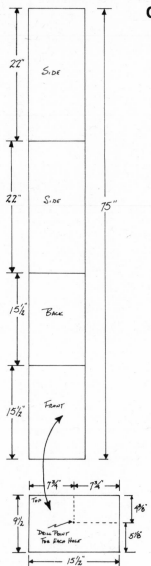

For basic box for each drawer.
1″ x 10″ pine
(¾″ x 9½″).

1″ x 10″ pine or ½″ plywood may be used for drawers.

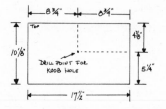

top drawer fronts.

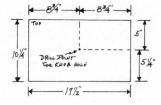

middle drawer fronts.

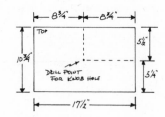

bottom drawer fronts.

CHANGING TABLE/BUREAU DRAWERS—ASSEMBLY

Glue, predrill and screw.
Sides between back and front.
Use 1¼″ #3 flathead screws for 1″ x 10″
pine.
Use 1″ #6 flathead screws for ½″ plywood.

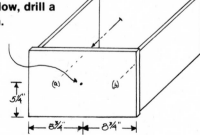

Premeasure on back of drawer fronts for attachment to drawer.

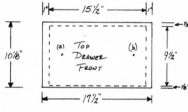

Glue drawer front to drawer, from the inside,
at points a and b, nail unit front to drawer front.

(Use ¾″ nails for ½″ plywood. Use 1″ nails
for ¾″ pine.)

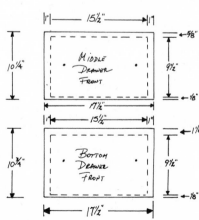

For knob, which will also serve to hold front
to drawer, measure as shown below, drill a
hole for knob bolt to slip through.

CHANGING TABLE DOORS—MATERIALS   ½″ plywood (A-D).

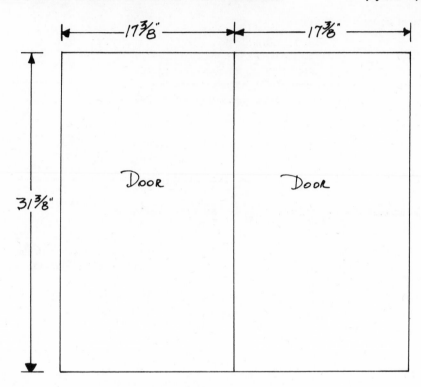

DOORS FOR CHANGING TABLE—PROCEDURE

1. Cut two doors 17⅜″ x 31⅜″ from ½″ plywood.

2. Place the hinges two inches up from bottom and down from top; use an awl and hammer to make a dent for the screws and screw the hinges onto the doors.

3. Brace against the cabinet and mark for the holes. Awl and hammer dents for the placement of the screws. Then screw the hinges onto the cabinet.

(I find it easier to put the hinges on the piece to be attached first, then its placement against the unit allows for more manipulable bracing and measuring for the hinge screws on the unit.)

CHANGING TABLE/CABINET—DOORS

For inset doors, use ½″ or ¾″ plywood.

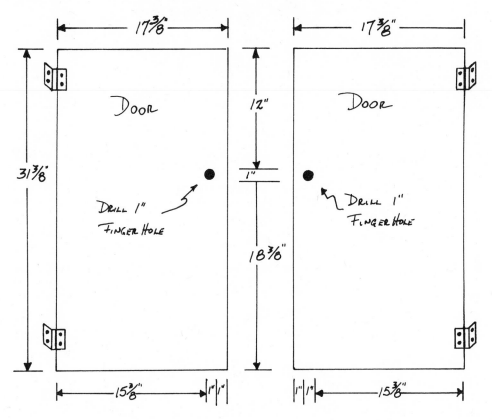

Attach hinges to doors first. Set top one 2″ down from top and the bottom one 2″ up from bottom edge.

Use offset hinges so they will screw into side of cabinet.

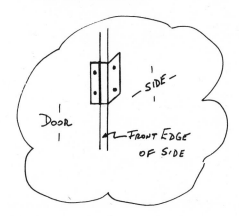

Project 4

BABY SEAT

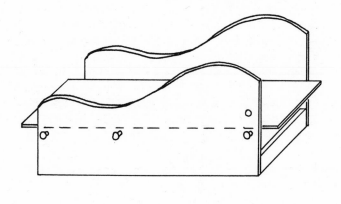

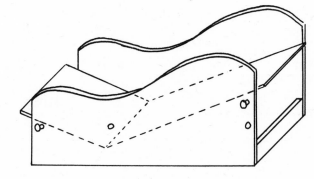

𝓌hether you build one of these baby seats or buy one, this is the only style I recommend. I had one exactly like this for my boys and never ceased appreciating it. It was a seat for being awake and playing and sometimes for eating, as well as an alternate bed, for it offered lying-down and sitting positions. However, the best feature was that it couldn't tip over, sideways or frontways. (I have watched two of my friends' babies throw themselves—and the seats they were strapped into— off the couch. No thanks, I don't like those thin plastic things with wire legs.

I remember that I used to wrap the baby all up in a cushy blanket and put him in the seat on the kitchen table so I could be with him, and he with me, while I did the kitchen chores. And he was safe. Yes, it was like a teeny portable crib.

You know how it is when you have something so perfect that you are constantly aware that it was a lucky find. That's how I feel about this baby seat. It was the very best of my baby things. I hope you and your baby will enjoy it as much.

My design is an improvisation. Mine of years ago had a track underneath for the seat to slide from flat to angled for sitting. That would be too hard to find or make, so I am using the dowel in and out instead, which will work as well, I believe.

Cover it with padded, quilted, waterproof baby-kind material and fashion a strap from some of the remnants. You could also attach rope or straps for carrying it.

BABY SEAT—PROCEDURE
1. Make an actual-size template for the sides, or draw a free-hand shape like the one shown.
2. Lay the template on the plywood and trace the shape onto the wood.
3. Cut out the first side.
4. Repeat steps 2 and 3 for the second side.
5. Measure for the back and cut out of plywood.
6. Measure for the seat and cut out.
7. From the length of 1″ x 3″, cut four 11″ lengths.

MAKE YOUR OWN BABY FURNITURE

BABY SEAT

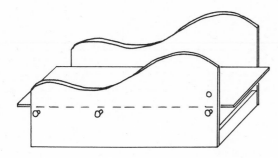

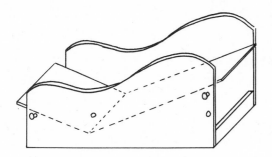

8. From the ½″ dowel cut three 13″ lengths.

9. From the 1¼″ dowel, cut six 1½″ lengths.

10. Sand all surfaces and edges.

11. Measure the inside of the sides and draw lines for the placement of the seat supports, as shown in diagram. (Repeat on the outside.)

12. Now, on the outside of the sides, measure for the dowel supports and drill the holes for them, from outside in.

13. Measure for the placement of the half-circle braces under the seat and screw them in.

14. Hinge the back and seat together.

15. On the outside of the sides, mark for two screws for each of the four 1″ x 3″ supports and predrill holes for the screws.

16. Carefully glue the supports in position, and after a few minutes stand the unit on one side and screw screws into top side and into top edges of supports.

17. Turn the unit over and repeat the process.

18. Using a table vise to hold the dowel, drill a 7/16″ hole, ½″ deep into each 1¼″ dowel length. (Place a piece of masking tape on the drill bit ½″ away from the flat cutting end to give you a guide showing when you've drilled ½″ in.)

19. Shave the ends of the ½″ dowels so they fit snugly into the 1¼″ dowel plugs.

20. Glue a plug on only one end of each ½″ dowel and put the dowels and other three plugs aside.

21. Cover the seat with some padded material. Cover the sides also, if you like.

22. Place the seat between the sides, slip one of the dowels through the holes at the feet, and through the half-circle braces under the seat. Glue a 1¼″ plug on the open end of the ½″ dowel. This dowel support is permanent.

When the seat is in sitting position, only the high position dowel at the head need be used, for the seat/back corner in the center will rest on the 1″ x 3″ angled supports.

When the seat/back is flat for sleeping, the head dowel is moved to the lower position and the center dowel is put in to hold the seat/back straight.

MATERIALS: ¼″ or ½″ plywood (A-D) leftovers.
or 1″ x 12″ (¾″ x 11½″) pine.

1″ x 3″ (¾″ x 2½″)

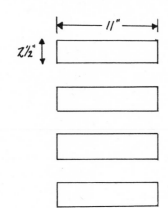

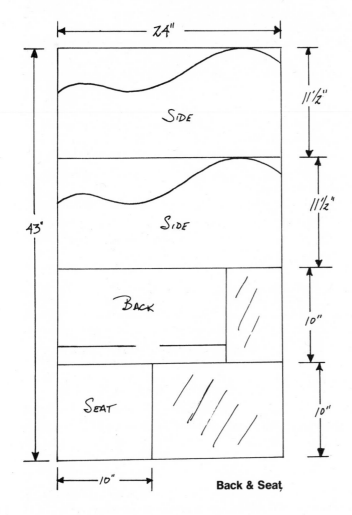

Back & Seat

½″-diameter dowels.

13″
(FOR PLYWOOD)

(3)

14″
(FOR 1″ x 12″)

1¼″-diameter dowels.

1½″ (6)

(2) ← (USE ¼″ SCREWS) ⅜″ radius, half-circle braces.

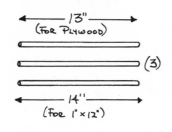

½″ HINGES (2)

If using plywood: 1″ #6 flathead screws.
If using 1″ x 12″: 1¼″ #6 flathead screws.

MAKE YOUR OWN BABY FURNITURE

BABY SEAT—ASSEMBLY

Measure as shown for placement of seat supports.

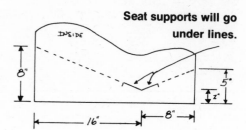

Seat supports will go under lines.

Measure and drill for dowel supports.

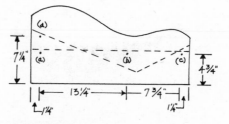

Drill holes using a ⅝" bore bit so dowels will slip through easily.

Drill point (d) for high back. ½" hole is up 7¼" from bottom.
Drill points (a) (b). Each is 4¾" from bottom.

Screw half-circle braces underneath seat.

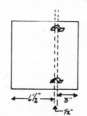

These braces will keep the seat in position. This dowel is permanent.

Hinge back and seat together *underneath*.

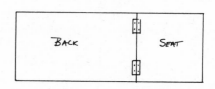

Be careful putting hinges on—check and be sure it will bend the proper way.

BABY SEAT—ASSEMBLY

Predrill for screws, through sides from
outside in.

Then probably the best thing to do is glue the
supports in place and let glue dry for 15 or so
minutes.

Carefully holding it together, turn on one side,
screw in, then turn on other side and screw
side to supports.

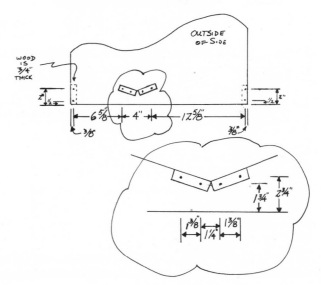

After the glue dries and seat is on its side,
then predrill through already drilled holes in
sides about ¼″ into supports.

Drill a 7/16″-diameter hole ½″ into 1¼″
dowels. Use long piece in vise. Don't cut into
1½″ length until after drilling.

Then shave the ends of the ½″ dowels so they
will fit in snugly. One end of two dowels will
have a permanent 1¼″ cap on them, so they
may be glued. Both end caps may be glued on
the foot end dowel, after the dowel has been
inserted from side to side, through the half-
circle braces under seat.

Project 5

CRIB/DESK

*T*he crib is perhaps the most important piece of furniture. It must be super-sturdy, because a growing baby is superpowerful, particularly when she wants to escape the confinement that the crib represents. The confinement is, of course, for the protection of the child. A baby on the loose could hurt herself in innumerable ways. However, a baby not on the loose could shake a flimsy structure to pieces in a matter of days. And in all honesty, a baby confined means a measure of peace for us who are grabbing a few extra winks for the day that faces us and our little cherub.

On the market are all manner of cribs. Yes, the flimsy, delicate, small crib for the early days, that must be replaced by the stronger, bigger crib for the stronger, bigger child. Why bother with two?

Because we require so much strength and protection from the crib, it becomes perhaps the hardest piece of furniture we will build. (No, Florence, it can't be slapped together!) However, a crib has a limited usefulness, two or three years a baby, times the number of babies. You may not know the result of that calculation yet. You may choose a crib that is a crib that is a crib. On the other hand, you may want convertibility. I include such an option.

Making the barred side of the crib is tricky. Thus, I have suggested you make only one side with bars, since the other side usually faces a wall. You might want to use a panel side similar to the one on the playpen, which can be cut from a piece of plywood, saving the doweling trip. Other alternatives may be sparks from your imagination, perhaps, and you will create your own design . . . and that's what this is all about, isn't it.

The mattress support can sit at three different levels. The highest position, the height of a desk, can also be an alternative to a cradle. The mattress support structure is attached with nuts and bolts, which add strength to the overall structure. The crib front hinges and folds open.

The framework eventually can be converted to a desk, simply by removing the doweled side. The mattress board is slotted for air circulation, and you would replace this with a solid piece for the desk. Some rolling cubes could be added underneath for storage. Boxes similar to the box on top of the changing table could be screwed to the back wall of the crib/desk for cubby storage. Your own ideas will enhance it further.

One final thought I want to share. Expose yourself to other women's babies at the "terrible twos" age. Watch them whiz their cribs across the floor. See them throw themselves over the rail. Listen to them shake, rattle, and roll, while they scream, "Mommy . . . OUT!" Yeah. It's coming! So, maybe you will nail the crib to the floor. Or build the sides higher. Or even add a lid? I remember that one of my sons used to throw himself over and out. I would try to awake before him, listen for him to wake, and run to him before he did the deed. The level of the mattress was its lowest. What could I do? God, I'm glad those days are behind me. Through all my baby-making days I used to envy my mother, who was deaf in one ear. She slept on her good ear . . . and slept . . . and slept, after one or two of the five of us were old enough to save the baby's life.

I also remember, thinking back on home, that we had a very long crib. I think one of my brothers slept in it until he was six. That's another alternative you might want to consider . . . a longer crib that could later become a youth bed just by substituting a half-doweled side. Or you could do a built-in, like the one suggested in back of the book. (Then, for sure, nothing would shake, rattle, and roll!)

So many choices. I wonder what my choice would be now? No, I don't. I would opt for convertibility . . . and higher sides . . . and probably now that I have some building experience . . . a built-in.

Construction comments: the crib was fun to do. It was the first time I tried to do a multidoweled structure. I had mixed emotions at first, worrying mostly if I could get the dowel holes straight up and down, or should I buy a drill press. (A drill press is a gadget that holds the drill straight and tight. You use a lever to raise or lower the drill. This way the drill is perpendicular to the surface you are drilling into. You can also get drill presses that give angular action.)

Yes, a drill press is super straightaway, and yes, many fine carpenters use them, but I am only a putterer. How often would I use this not-so-cheap gadget? So I decided to try it by hand.

I had had lots of drilling experience at this point and felt I could hold the drill fairly straight. If you feel edgy about it or have little experience drilling, practice a little. Drill some holes in scrap wood. Put a dowel in the holes and see how it sits. A little off is OK. You will notice that you can bend it a bit and when the whole structure is attached it will have come together nicely. However, if all

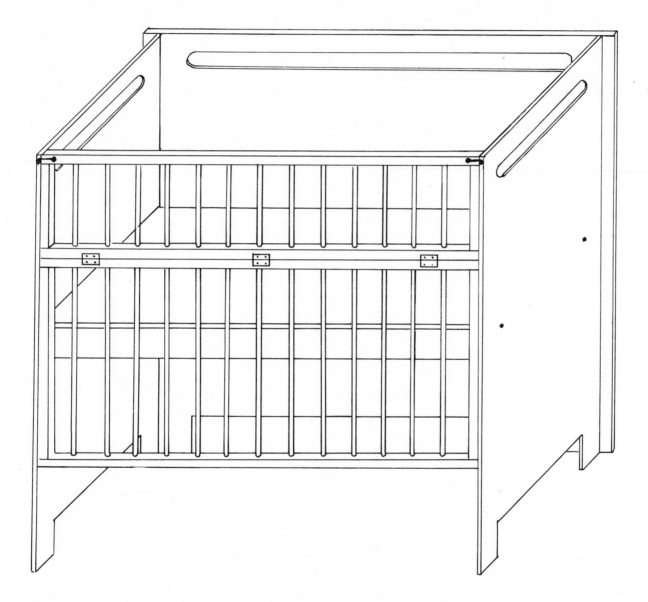

CRIB/DESK

your practicing evidences a serious problem, try to borrow a friend's drill press. (Borrow or rent when possible, rather than buy.)

The crib, as I said, is the most real, most vital piece of furniture for your baby. It took me two days, part of which was spent refiguring the plans as I built.

Mostly it's a job of sawing and drilling and snapping together. And it gives a great sense of accomplishment.

On the first day I cut and assembled the back, sides, base, and mattress board. I attached the board at desk height, pulled up a chair and sat down at the "desk." And I imagined the desk in use. I come from a large family. I was the oldest. Whenever my mother was pregnant, she referred to the unborn baby as "Imogene." I grew up thinking that "Imogene" meant baby-in-the-belly. As I sat at this new desk, too over the hill to have any more babies (thank God!), I whispered into the crib desk space, "Hello, Imogene, your crib will take you to college." Just then my younger son, Sam, came in. "Hey, mom, can I have that when the book is finished?" he asked. (So it turns out that though I didn't build him a crib twelve years ago, he's getting the desk. David, my older, had already had dibs on the changing table for a cabinet.)

The next day I grappled with the measuring for the dowels and the drilling. The dowels went in, this way and that, the frame around it joined. Here came the excitement! I held it against the desk. Behold: a crib! Fantastic! I hinged the two sections together and screwed the lower section into the sides. I felt wonderful. A crib. Imagine that. Do it. You'll feel wonderful, too.

CRIB/DESK—PROCEDURE
First piece of plywood
1. Measure for first 48″ cut, and cut out the back.
    Measure for second cut, and cut across 48″.
2. Measure for the side hooks, and carefully cut around hooks.
3. Measure for slots in back and side and cut them out. Start by drilling a hole big enough for the saw blade to fit through near the edge of the drawn diagram of the slot.
4. Measure for the feet cut-outs in the back and side, and cut them out.
5. On the back, measure for the thin slots, predrill a hole for the saw blade, and cut out the slots.

Second piece of plywod

6. Measure for the first 48″ cut, and cut across.

Measure for second cut, only 27⅜″ in, and cut only that far along the 48″ side.

Then from the other end, measure up 52 $\frac{1}{16}$″ and cut to meet the second cut.

7. Measure for the long slots in the side and mattress supports, drill a hole big enough for the saw blade to fit through, and cut out the long slots.

8. Measure for the feet cut-outs on the side, and cut out.

9. Measure for the side hooks, and carefully cut around them.

10. Measure sides for three levels of bolt holes and drill out with ⅜″ bit.

11. Attach sides to back by hooking together . . . just to see how it feels to start getting it together.

Remainder of materials

12. From the 2″ x 4″ cut two lengths 52⅛″ long and two lengths 24″ long.

13. From the ⅝″ dowels cut thirteen lengths 10⅝″ long and thirteen lengths 22⅝″ long.

14. From the baluster cut four lengths 52⅛″ long, two lengths 9⅞″ long, and two lengths 21⅞″ long.

15. Measure for the bolt holes on the 24″ lengths of 2″ x 4″ and drill holes using ⅜″ bit.

16. Corner-clamp the four corners of the base—the 2″ x 4″ sections—with the short pieces between the long pieces. Nail the corners together using 2½″ common nails.

17. Bolt the base onto the sides and back frame at the highest level. Lay the mattress board on top of the base . . . and you have a desk (with air holes).

18. Make yourself a drilling template for the placement of the dowel bars, where, except for the end areas, there is a space of three inches between every ⅝″ dowel. See the diagram, p. 89 for doing this.

19. Measure, using the template, for the dowel holes on the four long pieces of baluster. Use an awl to puncture a hole at the centered spot for the drill bit.

20. Measure ⅜″ in from the flat cutting edge of the drill bit and put a piece of masking tape on the bit to use as a guide to show you when you've drilled in deep enough. (See illustration, p. 89.)

21. Drill the ⅝″ diameter holes ⅜″ deep in the four pieces.

22. Get a friend to help you hold this together as you assemble.

Squirt some glue in each hole.

Place the dowels in the holes in one length. Holding it upright, squirt some glue in the holes in the second length and put the second length on top and work the dowels into the upper holes.

23. Predrill the corners for screws and screw the corners together.

24. Repeat steps 22 and 23 for the other doweled section.

25. Hinge the two sections together.

26. Clamp the lower section between the sides (see illustration, p. 91), predrill for the screws, and screw the doweled lower section to the sides.

27. At the upper front corner of each side, measure ¾″ down from top and ¾″ in from the front edge and puncture the measured point with an awl.

28. Clamp a 2″ x 2″ square of wood behind and drill a ½″ hole through the corner of the side. (The clamped wood behind will prevent the back surface from splintering.)

29. Apply glue inside the hole and insert a ½″-long, ½″-diameter dowel and let dry.

30. Measure down from the front edge ¾″ and drill a very thin hole through to the dowel. Screw the screw eye of the hook and eye lock into the hole. Do the same for the other corner. (The dowel plugs give the screw eyes something better to crab onto than the glued plywood sections, which might eventually separate after long use of that hook and eye.)

31. Screw the hook into the top bar to complete the lock. Hang the hook in the screw eye and hold it across the top bar, so that the hook's screw is pointed into the bar. Puncture the bar a bit with the screw, remove the hook from the screw eye and screw the hook in.

*Note! Be sure to use the type of hook with a spring lock—it's not one a child can open.

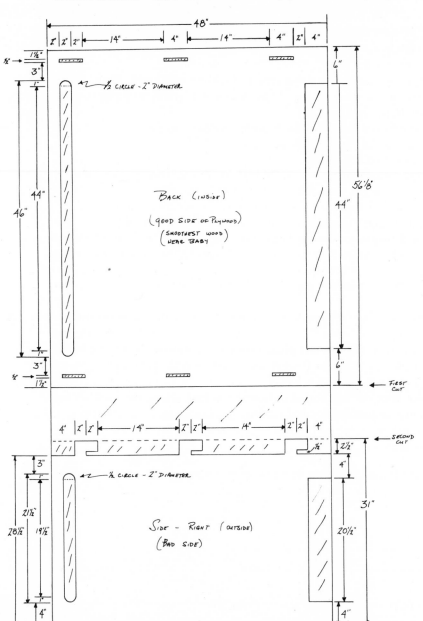

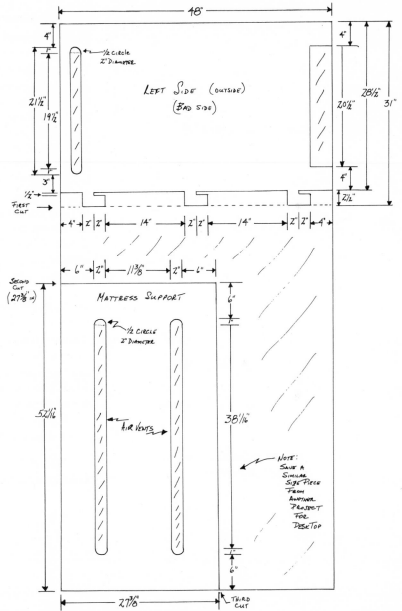

MAKE YOUR OWN BABY FURNITURE

2″ x 4″ (1½″ x 3½″).

52⅛″

3½″

(2)

(2)

24″

CRIB/DESK—MATERIALS

hinges: ½″ x 2″ (nonremovable pins).

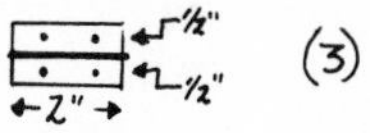

½″
½″
2″

(3)

⅝″ **dowels.**

(13)

10⅝″

(13)

22⅝″

nuts, bolts, washers.

3″

(4 SETS)

⅝″ DIAMETER

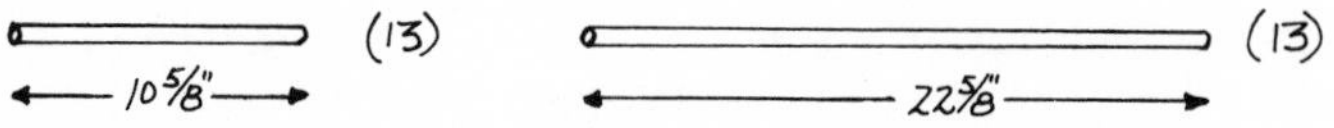

"baluster" (1-1/16″ x 1-1/16″).

52⅛″

(4)

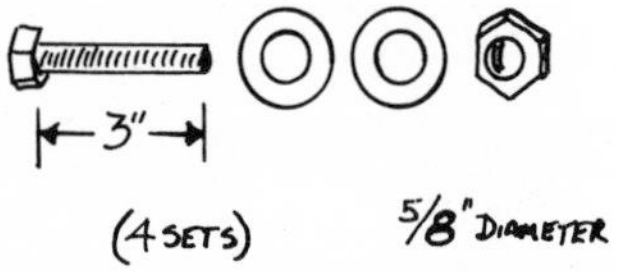

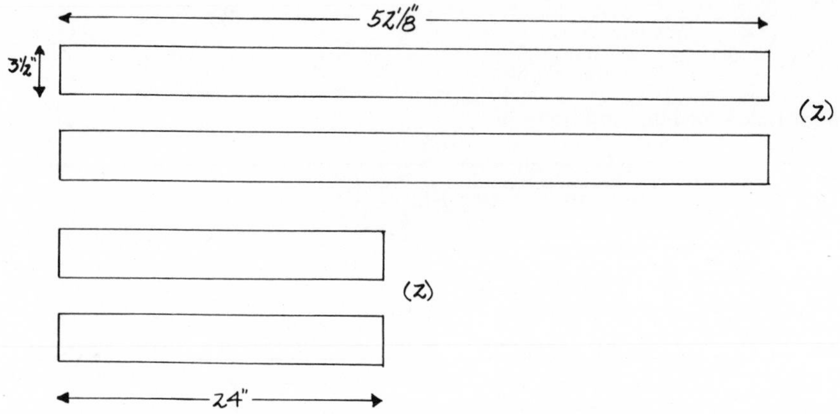

1¼″ #8 flathead screws.
2½″ common nails.

9⅞″

21⅞″

(2)

(2)

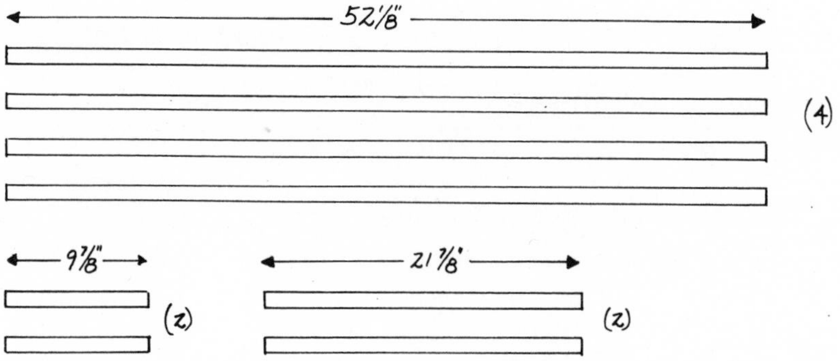

CRIB/DESK—ASSEMBLY

Measure for holes for nuts and bolts for
attaching base.

Measure, mark drill points with pencil,
puncture with awl.
Using ⅜″ bore drill bit, drill holes.

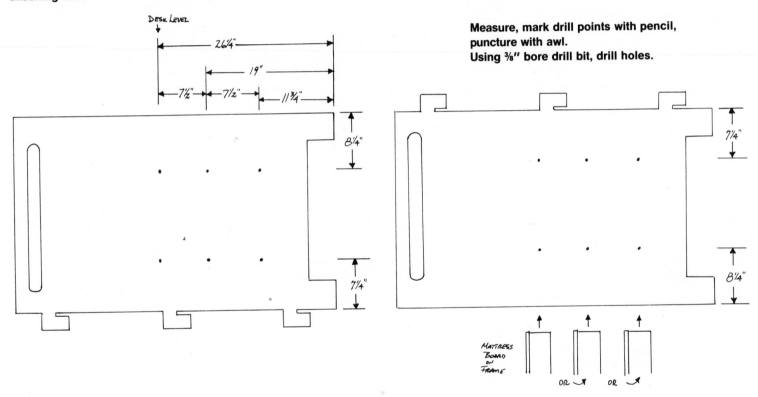

MAKE YOUR OWN BABY FURNITURE

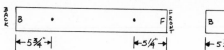

Mark short (24″) pieces of 2″ x 4″ as shown, puncture pencil point with awl, and drill ⅜″ holes (to later receive bolts). Also mark on wood B and F for "Back" and "Front."

Nail ends together using 2½″ common nails. Stand wood on 1½″-width edge on floor.

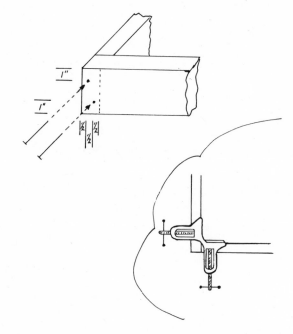

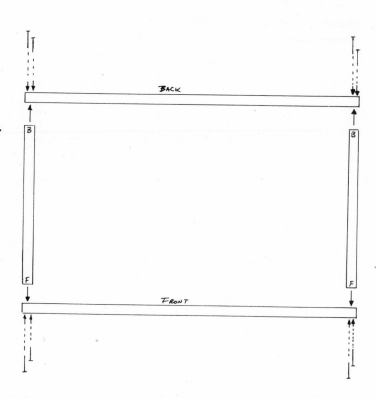

Clamp corners to square them before nailing.

CRIB/DESK—ASSEMBLY

1) Hook sides into back.

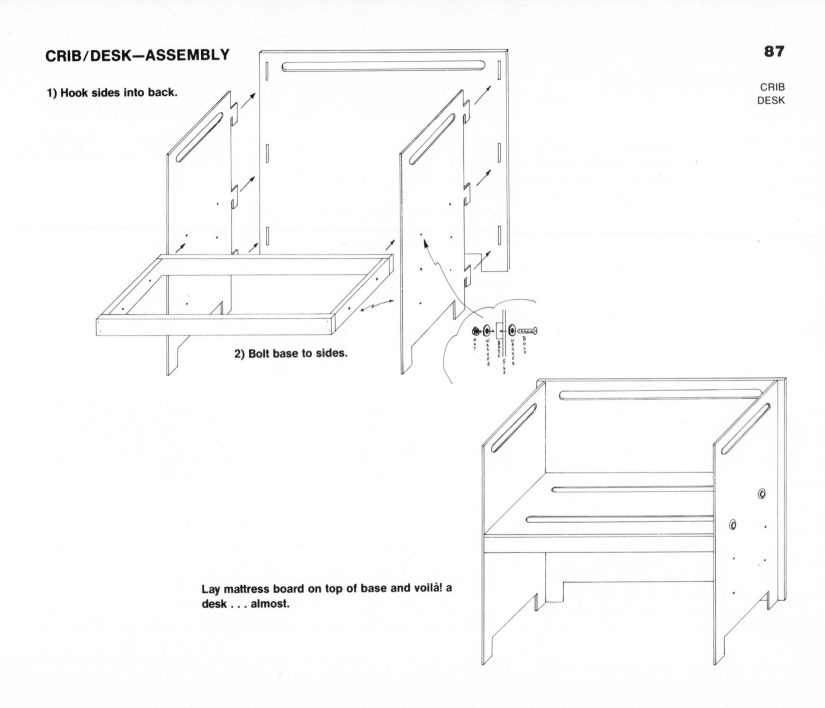

2) Bolt base to sides.

Lay mattress board on top of base and voilà! a
desk . . . almost.

MAKE YOUR OWN BABY FURNITURE

CRIB/DESK—ASSEMBLY

Crib side

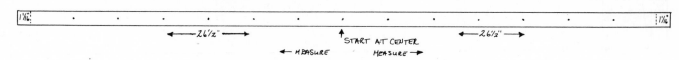

←— 26½" —→   START AT CENTER   ←— 26½" —→

←— MEASURE   MEASURE —→

Use template (see next page) to mark for drilling.

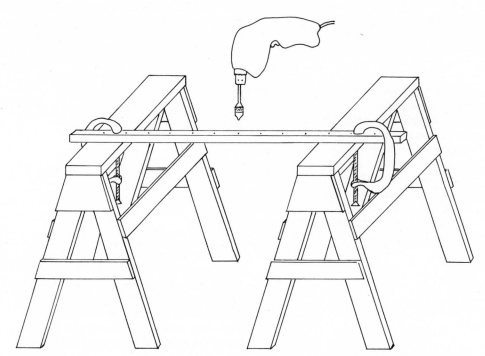

Clamp the baluster to sawhorses and drill holes.

Note: Practice drilling these holes in some scrap wood first and test holes by putting dowels in to see if they sit fairly straight up and down, then go for the real thing. Even if a little crooked, they will give a little when you put it all together.

CRIB/DESK—ASSEMBLY Template for marking dowel drill points.

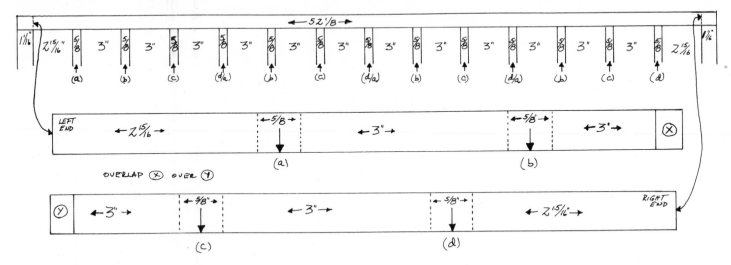

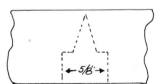

Make a template for marking the drill points for the dowel holes.

The template is half the width of the baluster frame wood. Lay it along one edge of the wood and make pencil dots on the wood at the arrow marks on the template. After you have completed one length of framing, moving the template as shown in the diagram to the left, go back, and puncture the wood through the pencil dot with an awl, providing a sure starting hole for the drill bit.

You will be using a ⅝" bore drill bit and should only drill ⅜" deep into the framing. In order to accomplish this accurately, wrap masking tape around the drill bore bit, ⅜" down from flat end, as shown in diagram below. Stop drilling as soon as you see the edge of the masking tape reach the wood.

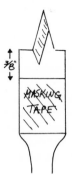

CRIB/DESK—ASSEMBLY
Doweled Crib Side

Squirt some glue in holes; put dowels into one strip.

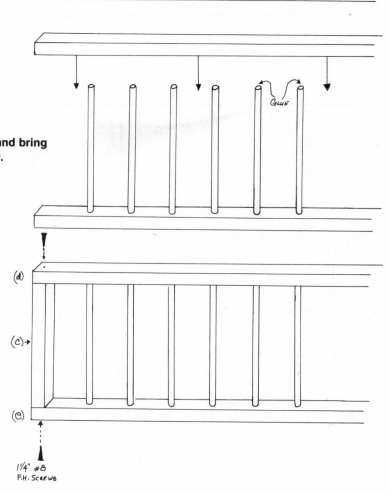

Squirt some glue on tops of dowels and bring top down onto dowels; push together.

c) Put end pieces of frame in between top and bottom and screw together.
d) For bottom of the top section predrill and screw together.
e) For larger bottom section of crib side, predrill and screw four corners.

1¼" #8
F.H. Screws

CRIB/DESK—ASSEMBLY

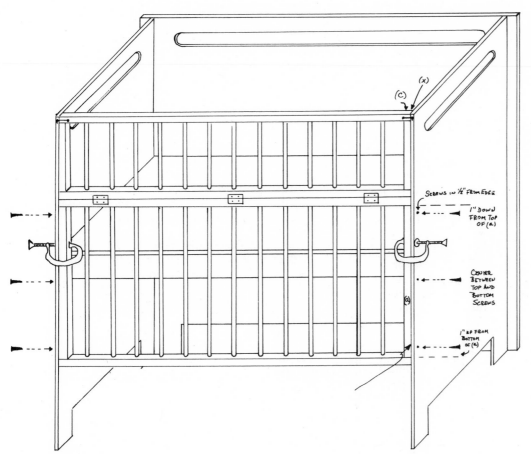

a) Hinge doweled sections (top and bottom) together.
Set left and right hinges 5″ from ends.
Center hinge is 25″ from each end.

b) Set doweled crib front against edges of sides, letting top of it hit flush at top edges of sides (x) and clamp; then screw together.

c) Screw side to doweled crib front. Predrill and use 1″ #6 flathead screws.

d) Screw eye hooks into top front edges of sides, and hooks at ends of top bar so the front can be locked. (See next page for details.)

Voilà! A crib!

SCREWS IN ½″ FROM EDGE

1″ DOWN FROM TOP OF (x)

CENTER BETWEEN TOP AND BOTTOM SCREWS

1″ UP FROM BOTTOM OF (x)

CRIB DOOR LOCKS—ASSEMBLY

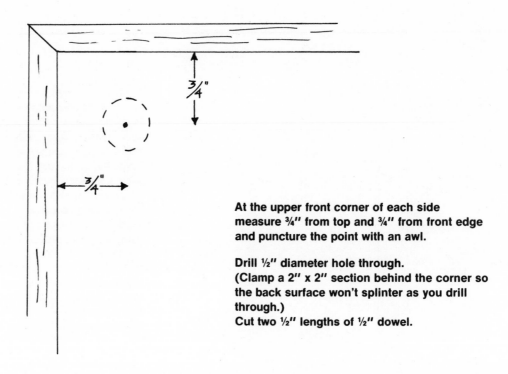

At the upper front corner of each side
measure ¾″ from top and ¾″ from front edge
and puncture the point with an awl.

Drill ½″ diameter hole through.
(Clamp a 2″ x 2″ section behind the corner so
the back surface won't splinter as you drill
through.)
Cut two ½″ lengths of ½″ dowel.

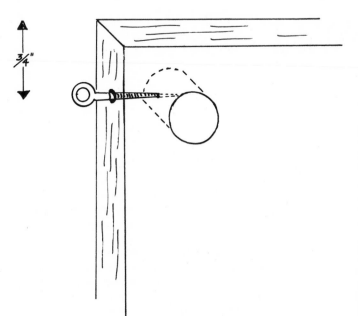

Apply glue inside holes and insert a ½"-long
½"-diameter dowel plug in each hole.
Plywood edges do not provide wonderful
security for screws and would tend to
separate after a while with abuse.
Since the screw eye for the hook and eye lock
will be screwed into the plywood edge, the
screw will go into the dowel plug, providing a
more lasting security.
Predrill into front edge of side, down ¾",
using very thin drill bit and screw eye.
Put the hook in the screw eye and hold it
across the top bar so that the hookscrew is
aimed at the bar. Puncture the bar with the
screw, remove the hook from the screw eye
and screw it in.
Do the same for the other corner.

Project 6

High Chair / Table Chair

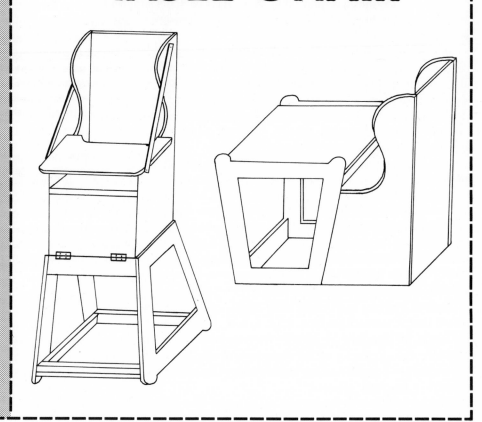

I don't know if they have this kind anymore, but if you are as old as I, you might remember the family high chair fondly. Certainly when I was baby-making years ago I often wished I'd had it for my children.

It was made of wood. In the center it was hinged so that it could convert from a *high* chair to a *low* chair and table. Nowadays we have either a high chair—high only—or a broad, low table with a chair set in, at a most uncomfortable height for feeding.

My brothers and sisters played on the "low" version of ours for hours. At mealtimes the chair was switched into high position and pushed close to the table. The high chair was an alternative to the playpen. Every variation of place to put the baby offers mommy some more free time!

The high chair, like the crib and playpen, must be sturdy, primarily because the child spends much time there . . . feeling trapped sometimes. So it, too, must be an unshakable fortress.

The high chair of our family was one with spindly, fancy-lathed legs. At the bottom was attached the table for play. This method of construction is difficult. It must be terribly precise to guarantee that it will remain in one piece. It also mandates tools I have not included for the more primitive project designs here.

Although the doweling for the crib must also be carefully done, the surrounding frame is the main source of support. In a high chair the spindly doweled legs would be the base support, similar to a dining room chair. How many of these chairs have you had that have become unglued, loose, and a pain to repair? So . . . no fancy doweled-leg high chair here.

Instead I offer a high chair built of pieces cut from plywood (fewer joints to loosen) that is convertible from high to low. When I designed it, I was surely in two heads, for the chair part comes from a plain version of early Americana. (I do truly love the simplicity of the furniture of our foremothers.) The bottom—the legs and table—comes from my today head of cutting shapes and structuring from plywood. A marriage of sorts.

The high chair was my biggest catastrophe of design. The table, when folded, must meet the chair at about the arm rest. I cut an inch here and there from standard lengths of high chairs to make it work. A friend was building it for me. "Something's wrong. It's too low." And so it was. A doll's high chair is what it looked like. Back to the drawing board I went, hearing that old cliché about haste and waste . . . and reminded about checking and rechecking measurements. (I used the plywood legs that were too short (14″) in a frame to hold plastic over the seeds I was growing indoors for the summer garden.)

HIGH CHAIR—PROCEDURE
1″ x 10″ board
1. Make a template for the high chair side guided by the pattern in the following pages.

Trace the pattern onto the board, and cut it out. Use a scroll saw blade which will cut rounded shapes better.

2. Again trace the pattern on the wood for the second side, and cut the second side out.

3. Measure for the chair back, and cut it out.

Measure for the chair seat, and cut it out.

Measure for the tray, and cut it out.

Measure for the seat brace, and cut it out.

4. Measure for the tray design, and cut it out from the tray section, using the pattern included.

½″ Plywood (odds and ends)
5. Measure for the table top, and cut it out.

6. Measure for the legs, using the pattern included, and cut them out.

Remaining wood
6. From the 1″ x 3″ cut two lengths of 14″.

7. From the baluster cut two lengths of 16″, two lengths of 17″, and two lengths of 14¼″.

8. Trim the 14″ 1″ x 3″ pieces angularly as illustrated, 13¼″ at the top and 13⅞″ at the bottom, which should yield an approximate angle of 83°.

9. Trim the 17″ baluster pieces angularly as illustrated, 16½″ at the top and 16¾″ at the bottom, which should also yield an angle of 83°.

10. Measure for the placement of the seat, back, and seat support. On the outsides, measure for the screw holes.

11. Glue the seat, back, and seat support to the sides and let dry.

HIGH CHAIR

HIGH CHAIR

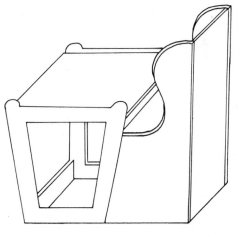

12. Laying the unit on one side, carefully drill through the side holes into the seat, support, and back, and screw in the screws. Turn it over and do the same on the other side.

13. On the inside of the legs, measure for the placement of the top and bottom supports, as shown in illustration, p. 101.

14. On the outside of the legs measure for the screws for the supports.

15. Predrill holes on the outside of the legs for all the supports and drill the holes.

16. Because of the angled corners you can't use corner clamps to hold this unit together as you work. My suggestion is to use thin nails 1″ long and do the following:

Glue and screw the 14¼″ side supports flush to the legs. Then glue the cross-supports in position on one side only and nail them together with the thin nails. Nail the nails all the way in on the unglued side and lay the unit on that side. Hammer the nails only partially through the other (top) side (the glued side) and work on this side first.

17. Predrill through each of the screw holes in the sides into the supports and, removing the nails, screw the side to the supports.

18. Turn the unit over onto the other side, separate the side from the support ends with a hammer, leaving the nails in the sides. Apply glue to the edges of the supports and then hammer back together, letting the nails protrude some, so they can be removed as you work. Repeat step 17 for this side.

19. Turn the leg unit upside down, lay the table top on the supports and predrill for the screws. Screw the screws in.

20. Predrill and screw the tray support arms to the tray.

21. Lay the tray in position on the arms of the chair and position the top of the tray arm supports against the top sides of the chair. Drill through the support and the side for the nut and attachment. Slip the nut through, with washer, from inside and tighten the bolt to the outside.

22. Hinge the chair to the legs.

23. Attach the hook-and-eye lock to the back.

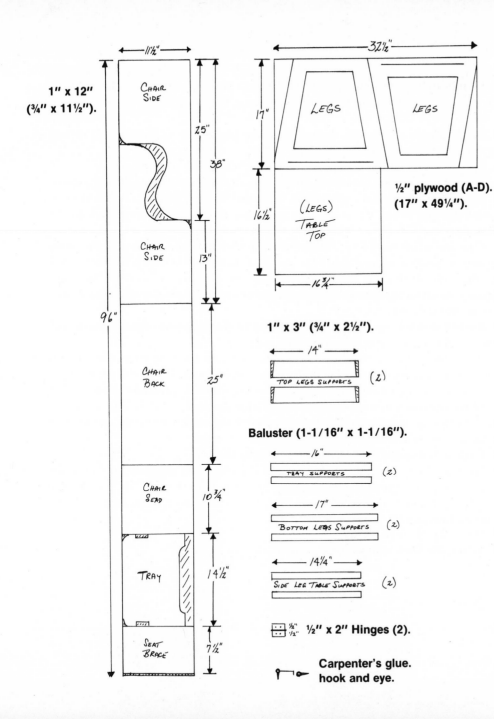

1" x 12"
(¾" x 11½").

1" x 12"

CHAIR SIDE

CHAIR SIDE

CHAIR BACK

CHAIR SEAT

TRAY

SEAT BRACE

32½"

LEGS   LEGS

17"

(LEGS) TABLE TOP

16½"

16¾"

½" plywood (A-D).
(17" x 49¼").

1" x 3" (¾" x 2½").

14"

TOP LEGS SUPPORTS   (2)

Baluster (1-1/16" x 1-1/16").

16"

TRAY SUPPORTS   (2)

17"

BOTTOM LEGS SUPPORTS   (2)

14¼"

SIDE LEG TABLE SUPPORTS   (2)

½" x 2" Hinges (2).

Carpenter's glue.
hook and eye.

HIGH CHAIR—MATERIALS

(See patterns for chair side, tray, and legs on following pages.)

1¼" #6 flathead screws.
1½" #8 flathead screws.
(2) ⅜"-diameter, 1½"-long bolts.
(2) nuts for ⅜" bolts.
(4) washers for ⅜" bolts.

MAKE YOUR OWN BABY FURNITURE

HIGH CHAIR—PATTERNS

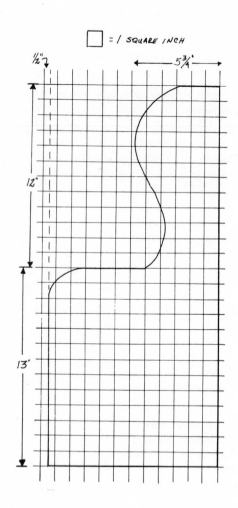

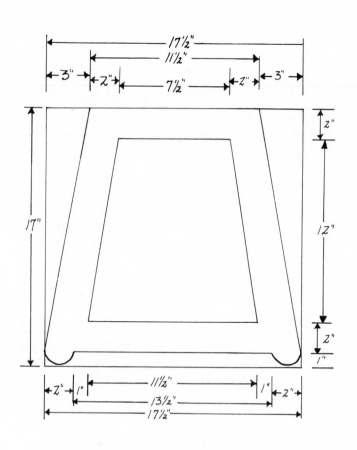

HIGH CHAIR—PATTERNS

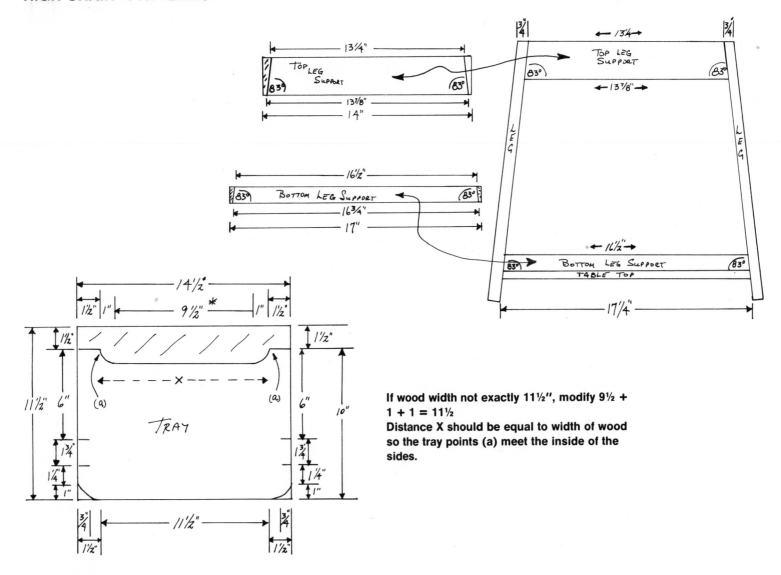

If wood width not exactly 11½″, modify 9½ + 1 + 1 = 11½
Distance X should be equal to width of wood so the tray points (a) meet the inside of the sides.

HIGH CHAIR—ASSEMBLY OF CHAIR

Measure for placement of seat.

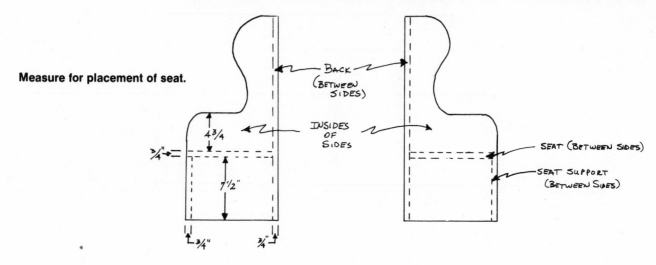

Attach sections.

Apply glue first, then screw.
1) Screw back to sides.
2) Screw seat to sides.
3) Screw seat support to sides.
Use 1¼" #8 flathead screws.

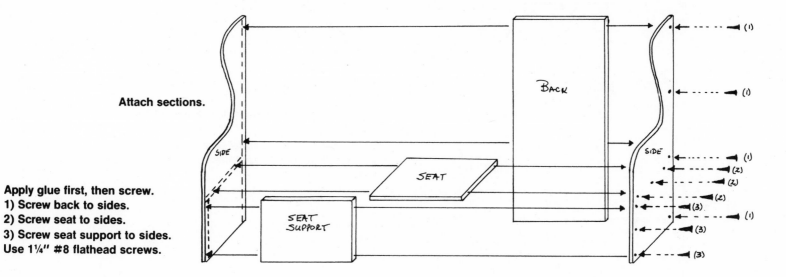

HIGH CHAIR—ASSEMBLY OF LEGS

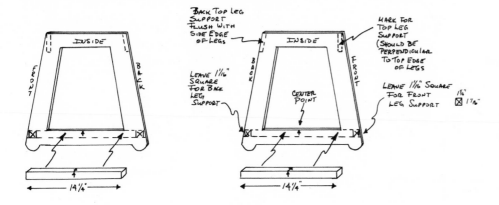

Mark center points and glue 14¼″ table supports flush to bottom line of opening. Screw in from outside to inside (one at each end, one at center).
1-1/16″ is allowed at each end to receive front and back bottom leg supports.

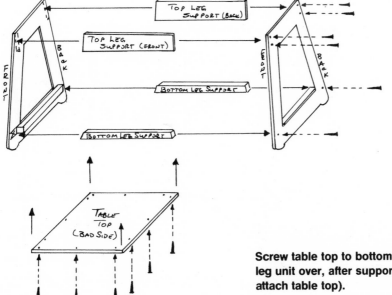

Screw top leg supports to sides. Screw bottom leg and table supports to sides.

Screw table top to bottom leg supports (turn leg unit over, after supports are attached, to attach table top).

MAKE YOUR OWN BABY FURNITURE

HIGH CHAIR—ASSEMBLY

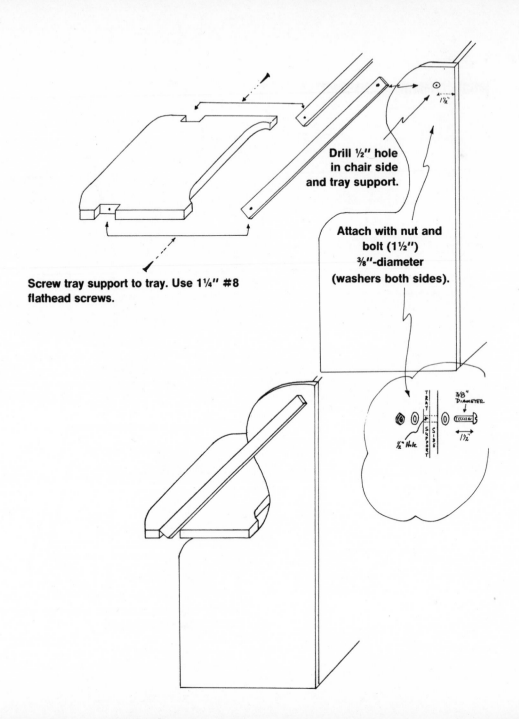

Drill ½" hole
in chair side
and tray support.

Attach with nut and
bolt (1½")
⅜"-diameter
(washers both sides).

Screw tray support to tray. Use 1¼" #8
flathead screws.

HIGH CHAIR—ASSEMBLY

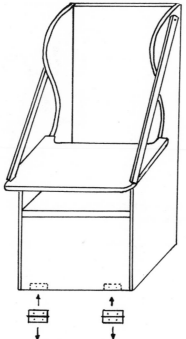

Hinge chair to legs.

Attach hook and eye in back center.

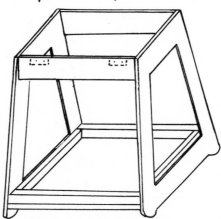

Project 7

PLAYPEN/ PLAYHOUSE

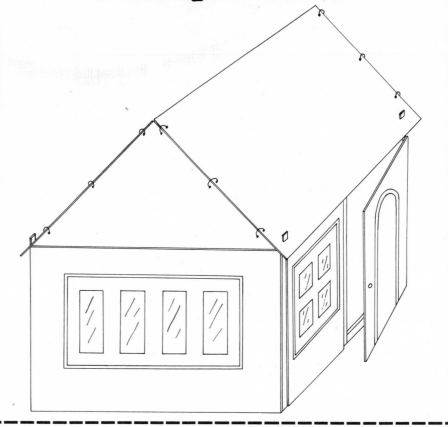

The playpen presents the biggest dilemma. It seemed to me impossible to recycle into some future usefulness. At first I started out suggesting the conventional style, wooden bars, with the modification that two sides be mesh if you like, marrying the sturdy climbing bars with the lightness of the mesh sides. But I remained bugged by its obsolescence. Further, it is an expensive item to become useless so soon.

Then, recently, I had a vision, kind of like a double exposure in my mind. I saw the playpen I was working out and then suddenly I saw this playhouse over it. Just like that. What a wonderful idea. After all, the basic box structure for the playpen is just what you need for a little playhouse. Fantastic! And I raced back to the drafting table to work it out.

Forget the blasted bars and all the work to do them. Use panels. Cut shapes out of the panels—none larger than three inches so little heads don't get caught. And when the playpen is outgrown, put the child right back into it! Only this time the panels are replaced with house-side panels and a whole new environment is created. And she will probably move half her world in there with her . . . the stuffed animals, a small chair, a table maybe . . . tea parties in the playhouse. Wow. I want to be a kid again myself.

Well, anyhow, now I present this to you as an alternative to the conventional playpen. And I also present the conventional one, too. If you prefer to create the slatted-bar playpen, the basic structure is still the same. The insertion of dowels is similar to what's done in the crib project earlier. And, as I have suggested here, you can have one doweled side and panels on the other three sides.

The playpen is a large and cumbersome thing to leave around all the time, particularly if you are cramped for space. Furthermore, you may want to transport it . . . to nana and poppie's house (or whatever you call the grannies) . . . so it should fold.

I remember, now, that I used to drag mine to the beach. I fitted it up, folded, with a set of wheels strapped on like those used on luggage, and dragged it with one hand and held the baby in the other arm . . . many years ago when I was younger and stronger and hungering for a day at the beach no matter the price.

Now they go to the beach by themselves . . . THANK GOD! and I sit out back with a vodka and orange and feel free.

So anyway, this piece of baby furniture is vital to your freedom, as it is also a large free world for your growing baby.

I have my own prejudices about all of the things herein and have naturally incorporated them in my designs. For instance, I don't really like mesh sides because they seem not to offer a sturdy hold for a climbing baby, but I do like the idea of one doweled side. Not only do dowels offer a stronger hand-holding climbing effect, but they are a hard surface on which to attach things like the gadget box and other toys to intrigue and absorb the baby while you are busy doing other things . . . or just doing the "usual" bonbons and TV thing that mommies do at home . . . don't we!

It's not the easiest project, mostly because of the sanding and, yes, the doweling of the one side; but if you've done the crib, you're a pro, and there ain't nothin' you can't do now!

One more opinionated measure of advice. I mothered two very active boys, who are now twelve and fifteen, still robust and active. And how many days I wish I could throw them back into the playpen, one turned upside down as in *Please Don't Eat the Daisies* (Jean Kerr fashion). When I read that book, too late to be of any help to me, for my guys were no longer toddlers, I thought, now there's one smart mommy! Why didn't I think of that! So I offer this thought to you. If you expect to have a hellion on your hands, build the playpen a bit higher, and on those very bad days when she is climbing out, whiny, bored, turn it upside down. Just the novelty of the new environment will hush her for a long while. The gadget box in reverse may add some additional intrigue. You might even have time for a short nap. If a friend drops in and is astonished, hand her a copy of *Daisies* and share a quiet cup of tea.

Take it from here with the modifications . . . and have fun.

PLAYPEN—PROCEDURE

Baluster

1. One at a time, measure for and cut four lengths of 42⅛″, fourteen lengths of 24″, eight lengths of 20″, two lengths of 36″, and four lengths of 15″.

⅝″ dowel (if you are doweling one side)

2. One at a time, measure for and cut ten lengths of 24¾″.

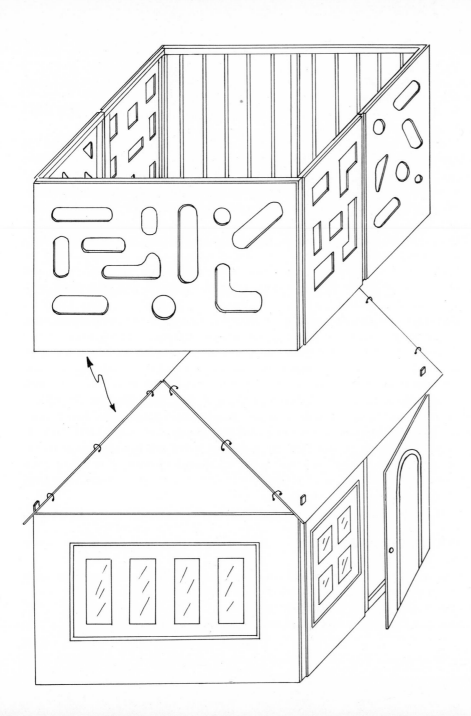

PLAYPEN/PLAYHOUSE

Masonite, first piece

3. Measure for the first 48″ cut, and cut out first section.
Measure for the second 48″ cut, and cut out second section.
Measure for the third 48″ cut, and cut out third section.

Masonite, second piece

4. Measure for the first 48″ cut, and cut out first section.
Measure for the second 48″ cut, and cut out second section.
Measure for the third 48″ cut, and cut out third section.
Measure for the fourth 48″ cut, and cut out fourth section.

5. Measure for the smaller pieces and cut them out of the larger sections. Put these aside until after the assembly of the basic structure. Measure for the handholds in the floor and cut them out.

6. Corner-clamp the pieces of the frame for the long side, predrill, and screw the pieces together. Do the same for the second long side only if you are not doing one doweled side.

7. If you are doing one doweled side, do the following for that side:

a) Make yourself a drilling template for the dowel holes on the two long pieces of baluster. (Use the guide in the crib section.) Use an awl to puncture the ten holes for the drill bit.

b) Measure ⅜″ in from the flat cutting edge of the drill bit and put a piece of masking tape on the bit to use as a guide to show when you've drilled deep enough. (See the illustration of this in the crib section.)

c) Drill the ⅝″ holes ⅜″ deep in the two long lengths of baluster.

d) Squirt glue in each hole of one length and insert the dowels. Squirt glue in the holes of the other length and place it on top of the standing dowels and work them into the holes.

e) Predrill the corners for the screws and screw the corners together.

8. Corner-clamp the pieces of the frame for the short side, and predrill and screw the pieces together. Do the same for the other three short sides.

9. Hinge the six sections of the frame together.

10. Predrill for, glue, and screw the floor supports under the floor pieces, from the masonite into the supports.

11. Screw the hinges onto the floor pieces.

12. Hinge the floor to the bottoms of the long sides of the frame.

13. Draw the designs of your choice on the panels. No opening should be greater than a baby's head can fit through. (Three inches is a good maximum.)

14. Cut out the design. First, predrill a hole large enough for the saw blade, then saw the shape out.

15. Using C-clamps at the top of a panel, clamp a panel to a side, predrill, and screw it into the side. Repeat for all the panels.

PLAYHOUSE

16. When the time comes to transform the playpen into a playhouse, cut the roof panels from a third piece of Masonite, and use the side panel cut from the second cut earlier or cut a new panel.

17. From a fourth piece of Masonite cut out panels similar to the panels from the first piece of Masonite, one large panel and four small panels, similar to steps 3 and 5.

18. Draw the house designs on the panels and cut out windows and door.

19. Remove the floor of the playpen.

20. Detach the playpen panels. If you have one doweled side, leave it there and either put a panel over it or leave it open as doweled.

21. Attach the house panels as in step 15.

22. Cut the rectangular corner cut out of the 2 large roof panels.

23. Drill holes in the roof panels for the rope ties, and tie the panels together.

24. At each corner, as shown in illustration, p. 119, screw on 4″ lengths of baluster. These corner posts will hold the roof in position.

25. Sit the roof on the house, slipping it over the corner posts.

MAKE YOUR OWN BABY FURNITURE

**PLAYPEN/PLAYHOUSE—
MATERIALS**

1½″ #8 flathead screws.
¾″ #6 flathead screws.
Carpenter's glue for dowels.

⅝″ dowels—if you do one doweled side.

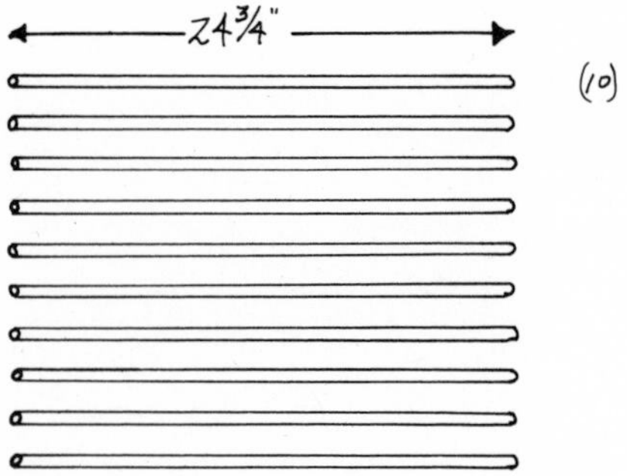

24¾″ (10)

Baluster (1-1/16″ x 1-1/16″) for framing.

42⅛″ (4)

24″ (14)

20″ (8)

Baluster for floor

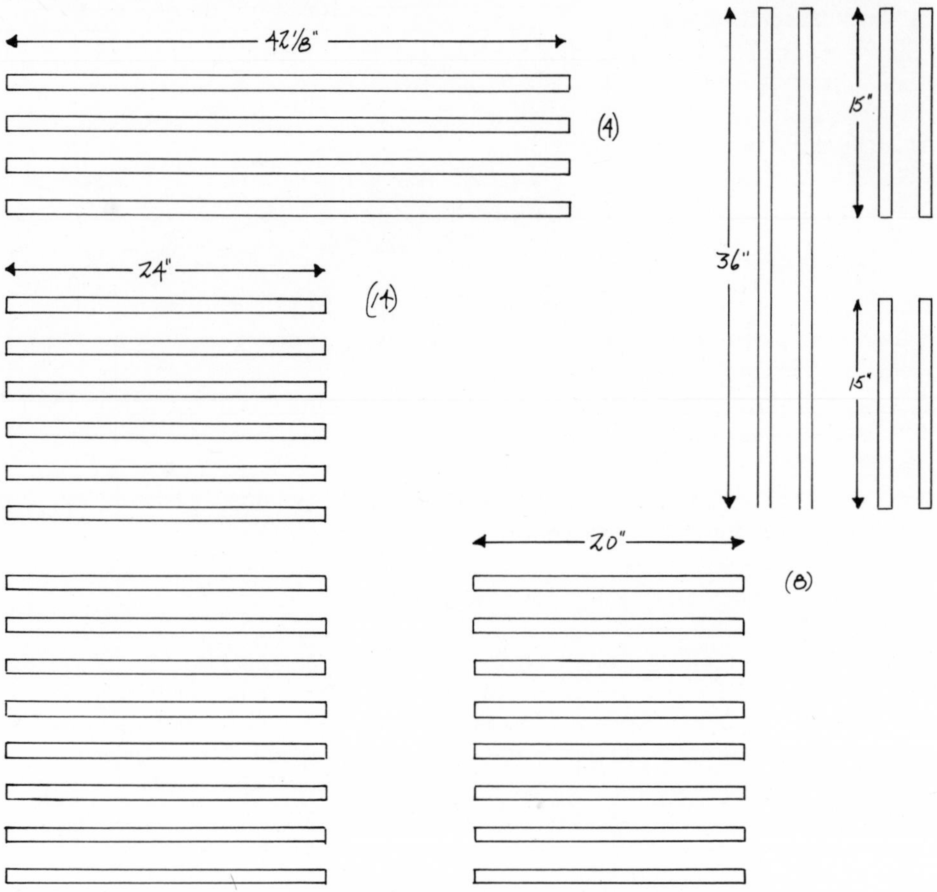

36″

15″

15″

1″ x 2″ hinges.

1″
2″
—OR— 1″
(12)

USE 1″x2″
OR
1″x1″
HINGES

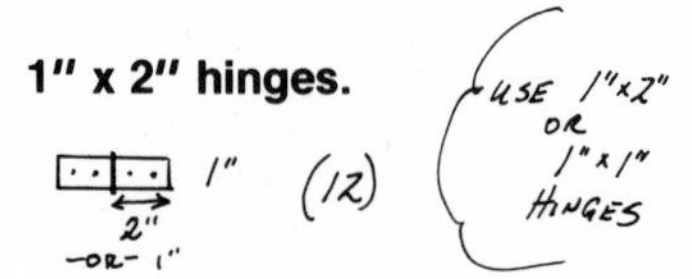

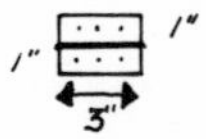

3″ x 1″ hinges.

1″
1″
5″

³⁄₈″-thick Masonite 4′ x 8′.

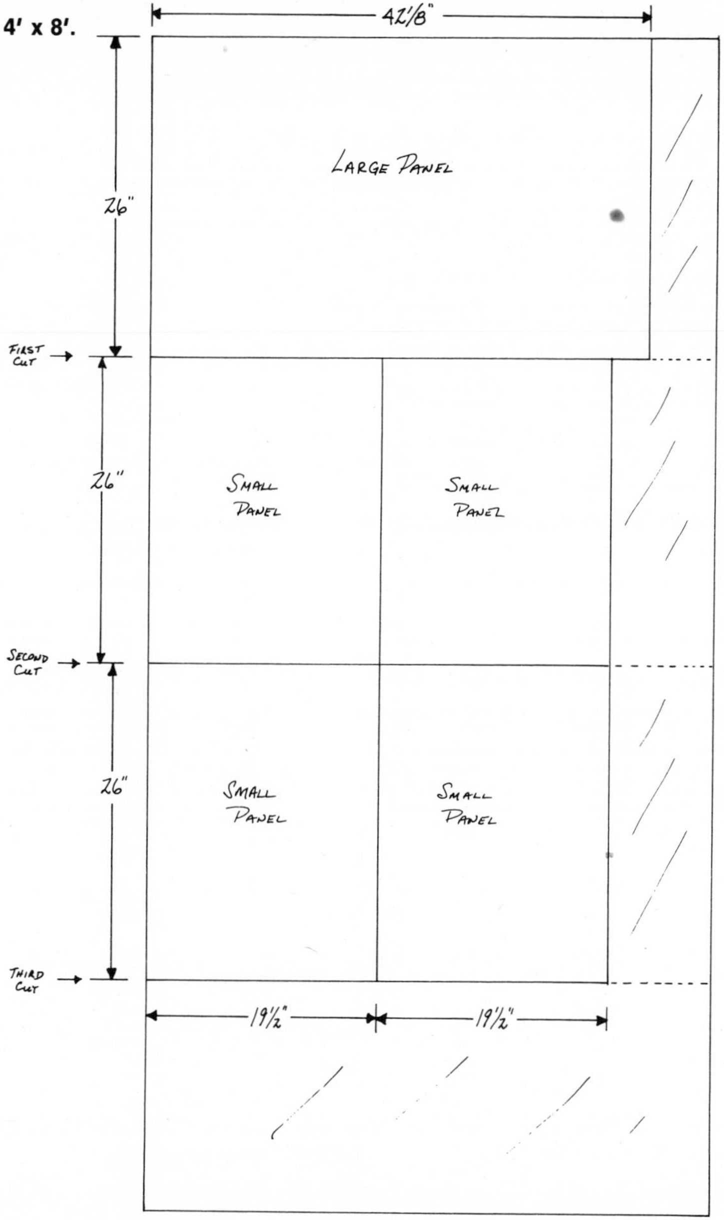

42⅛″

LARGE PANEL

26″

FIRST CUT →

SMALL PANEL   SMALL PANEL

26″

SECOND CUT →

SMALL PANEL   SMALL PANEL

26″

THIRD CUT →

19½″   19½″

Panels for playpen with one doweled side. For a playpen with 2 large panels—without doweled side—another panel 26″ by 42⅛″ will be needed.
Also, for *playhouse* these sizes plus one more for second large panel are needed.
(See next page for extra Masonite for second large panels.)

⅜"-thick Masonite 4' x 8'.

Roof panels.   ⅜"-thick Masonite 4' x 8'.

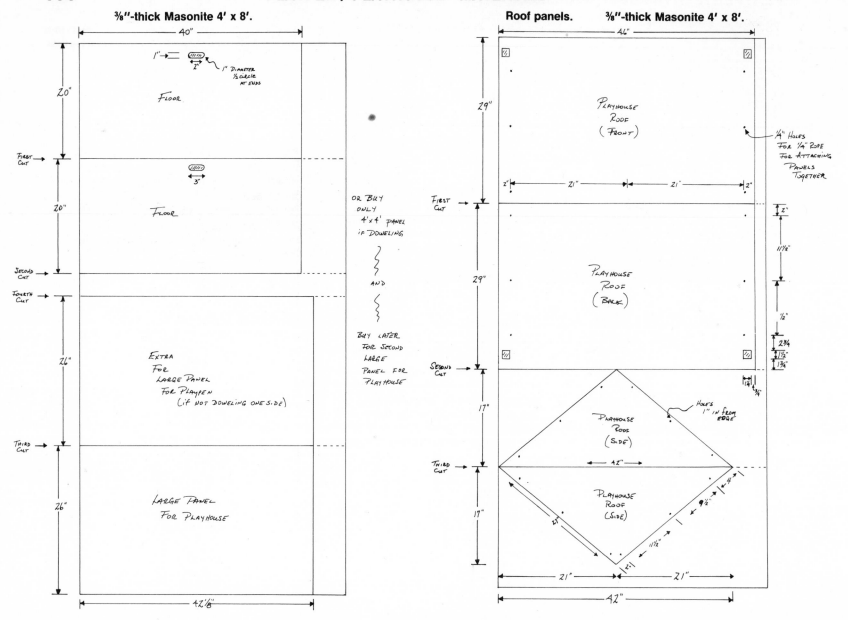

40"

20"

FLOOR

1" → ⊏
2"
1" DIAMETER
½ CIRCLE
AT ENDS

FIRST CUT →

20"

FLOOR

3"

SECOND CUT →

FOURTH CUT →

26"

EXTRA
FOR
LARGE PANEL
FOR PLAYPEN
(IF NOT DOWELING ONE SIDE)

THIRD CUT →

26"

LARGE PANEL
FOR PLAYHOUSE

42⅛"

OR BUY
ONLY
4' x 4' PANEL
IF DOWELING

AND

BUY LATER
FOR SECOND
LARGE
PANEL FOR
PLAYHOUSE

46"

29"

PLAYHOUSE
ROOF
(FRONT)

¼" HOLES
FOR ¼" ROPE
FOR ATTACHING
PANELS
TOGETHER

FIRST CUT →

2"   21"   21"   2"

29"

PLAYHOUSE
ROOF
(BACK)

2"

11½"

½"

2¾"
1½"
1¾"

SECOND CUT →

¼" ¾"

17"

PLAYHOUSE
ROOF
(SIDE)

HOLES
1" IN FROM
EDGE

42"

THIRD CUT →

17"

PLAYHOUSE
ROOF
(SIDE)

4"

9½"

11½"

27"

21"   21"

42"

Frame—long side (2).

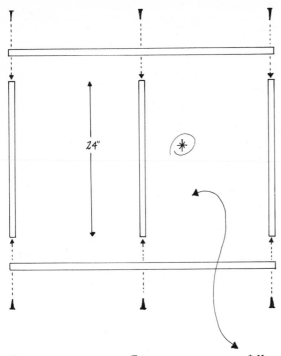

24"

**Attach short (24") pieces within long pieces
(42⅛").**
**Use corner clamps; predrill and screw
together using 1½" #8 flathead screws.
Also, countersink holes or use 3-in-1
combination bit.**

*** If you choose to do one doweled side, then
first predrill for ⅝" dowels, insert them before
screwing in the 24" cross-pieces.
See the crib section for the doweling
procedure.
The layout in half of the large frame will be:**

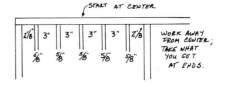

24"

Short sides (4).

MAKE YOUR OWN BABY FURNITURE

Screw the floor supports (a), (b), (c) to the
two floor sections (from floor into support),
and screw hinges into floor pieces.
Hinge the 6 sections of the frame together.
Then hinge floor on.
(Use ¾" #6 flathead screws for hinges.)

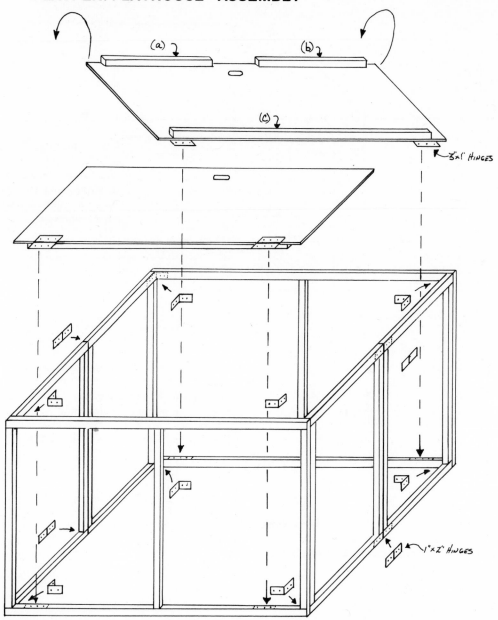

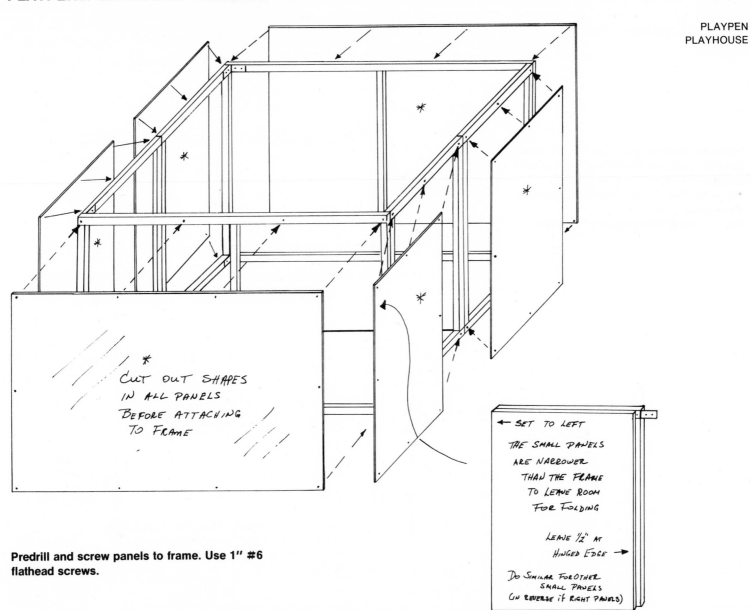

* CUT OUT SHAPES
IN ALL PANELS
BEFORE ATTACHING
TO FRAME

Predrill and screw panels to frame. Use 1″ #6 flathead screws.

← SET TO LEFT

THE SMALL PANELS
ARE NARROWER
THAN THE FRAME
TO LEAVE ROOM
FOR FOLDING

LEAVE ½″ AT
HINGED EDGE →

DO SIMILAR FOR OTHER
SMALL PANELS
(IN REVERSE IF RIGHT PANELS)

PLAYPEN/PLAYHOUSE—PANEL TEMPLATES

□ = 1 SQUARE INCH

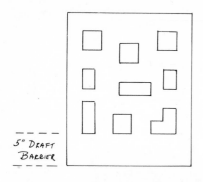

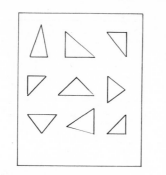

5" DRAFT BARRIER

Design any kind of panel you like—however, be sure no openings are greater than 3″ so that heads cannot get stuck.

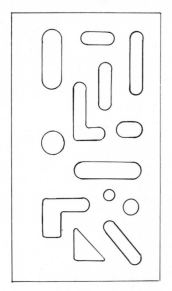

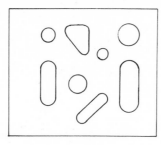

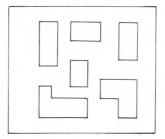

PLAYPEN/PLAYHOUSE—PANELS FOR PLAYHOUSE

□ = 1 SQUARE INCH

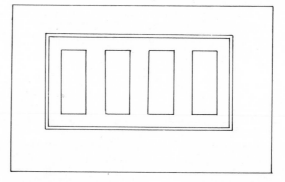

Cut out windows 4″ x 10″. Print border around.

Paint on flower pots, etc.

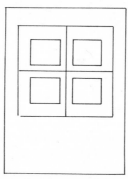

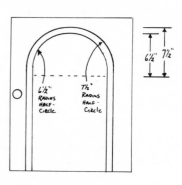

6½″ 7½″

6½″ RADIUS HALF-CIRCLE

7½″ RADIUS HALF-CIRCLE

**Make door 2″ shorter than side panel; hang lower because of 2″ overhang on roof.
Paint onto door section a door and door knob design.**

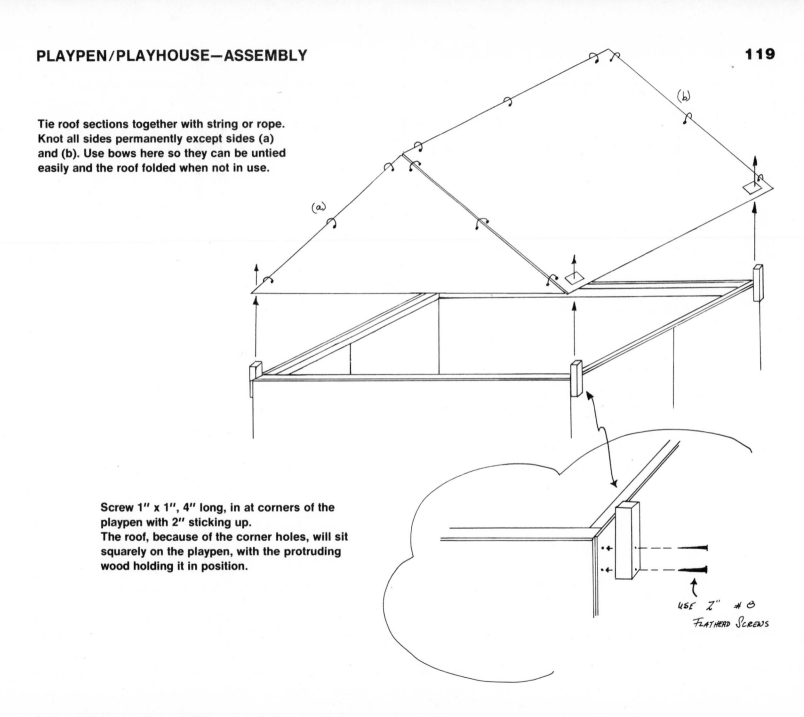

Tie roof sections together with string or rope. Knot all sides permanently except sides (a) and (b). Use bows here so they can be untied easily and the roof folded when not in use.

Screw 1″ x 1″, 4″ long, in at corners of the playpen with 2″ sticking up.
The roof, because of the corner holes, will sit squarely on the playpen, with the protruding wood holding it in position.

USE 2″ #8
FLATHEAD SCREWS

Project 8 SWING AND FRAME

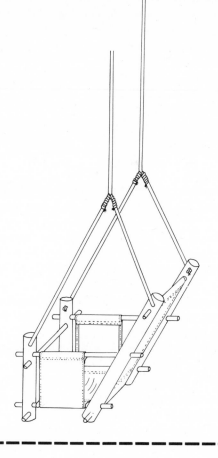

I guess I harp on this throughout, that the more places to move the bored baby, the more peace for mommy, but it's true. (A baby having fun, being stimulated, isn't crying, that's why.)

A swing, hung in a doorway where there's a big chunk of wood into which to screw a big screw eye to hold the swing's rope, is a great baby place.

If you are any good at sewing a strong stitch, the swing is an easy gadget to make.

Also included is a frame to hold the swing indoors or outdoors. If you have the room indoors, it might be preferable to the doorway swing, which would probably have to be removed when not in use.

A swing with a high back adds one more nicety . . . the baby may rock herself to sleep—wonderful!

SWING—PROCEDURE

1. From the 1½″ dowel cut two lengths of 9″ and two lengths of 15″.

2. From the ⅝″ dowel cut four lengths of 15″, two lengths of 11″, and two lengths of 14″.

3. On the 15″ lengths of 1½″ dowel measure for the two perpendicular ⅝″ holes. Notice in the illustration of the first left hole that the ⅝″ hole is ½″ away from the edge. Thus the drill point would be ½″ + ½ (of ⅝″), or ½″ + 5/16″ = 13/16″. Drill holes.

4. Next, on the same two dowels, measure for the angular dowel holes. These holes will go through the wood perpendicularly to the first three holes, but will be drilled on an angle. A suggestion for accomplishing a 60° angle of drilling is this: after marking the two points, lay the dowel on a piece of paper marked for a 60° angle. Make the 60° line on paper long enough to have the angle visible when you lay the dowel on top. With a pencil, sketch the angle onto the dowel. Then as you drill you can see if the drill bit is following the angle as it goes through. Use a table vise to hold the dowels as you drill.

5. On the ⅝″ dowels, measure for the holes for the cotter pins. Use a drill bit slightly larger than the cotter pin.

MAKE YOUR OWN BABY FURNITURE

SWING

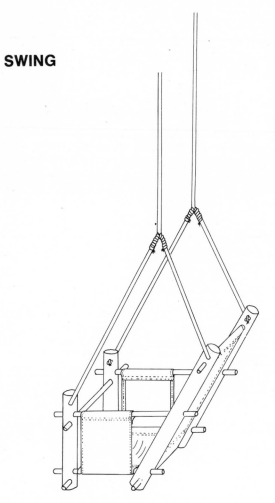

6. Cut, baste, and sew the fabric for seat and back.

7. Slip the 15″ lengths of ⅝″ dowel through the ends of the back material, and slip the dowel ends through appropriate holes in the 15″-long 1½″ dowels, as shown in the illustration. Secure with cotter pins.

8. Slip the 11″-long ⅝″ dowels through seat-ends material, and the 14″-long ⅝″ dowels through the arm/wraparound seat material ends.

9. Insert the 11″-long dowel ends into the 1½″ dowels, then the 14″-long dowels into the 1½″ dowels and secure with cotter pins.

10. Insert the remaining 15″-long dowel handlebar and secure with pins.

11. String the rope through the top holes in the 1½″ dowels and tie, so that the swing hangs level.

12. Screw two large open or closed screw eyes into the top of a doorway's woodwork, spaced 13″ apart and equally spaced from the corners of the doorway.

13. Put the swing rope through and decide where to make the final knots, based on the swing height you desire.

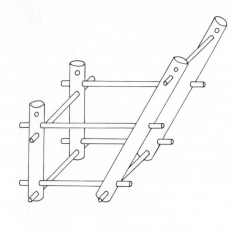

SWING—MATERIALS

1½"-diameter dowel.

⅝"-diameter dowel.

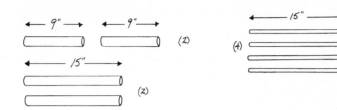

Also: 1¼" cotter pins.
20' ½" rope.
1 yard of canvas at least 2' wide.

SWING—ASSEMBLY

= 1 SQUARE INCH

9" dowel:

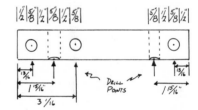

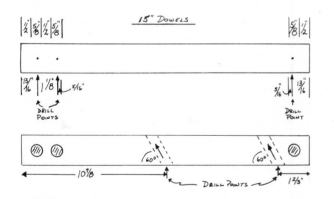

Drill holes in 1½" dowels to receive ⅝" dowels and rope.

Drill holes in ⅝" dowel for cotter pins.

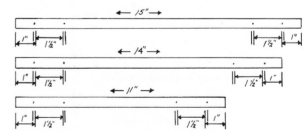

MAKE YOUR OWN BABY FURNITURE

SWING—MATERIALS

Canvas seat: 14″ x 7¾″ seamed to 11″ x 5¾″.

☐ = 1 SQUARE INCH

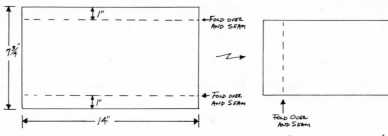

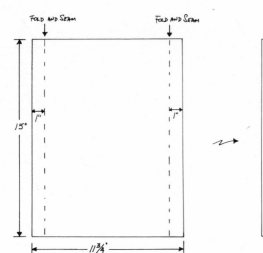

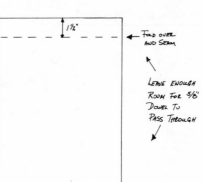

Back: 15″ x 11¾″ seamed to 12″ x 9¾″.

Arm/wraparound seat: 25″ x 7″ seamed to 22″ x 5″.
With some of the leftover material make a strap to hold baby in.

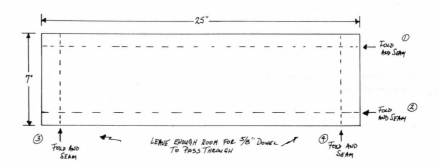

SWING—ASSEMBLY

Assemble, putting cotter pins through ⅝″ dowels on both sides of 1½″ dowels in *all* cases, as shown in 2 samples (a), (b) and just by arrows elsewhere.

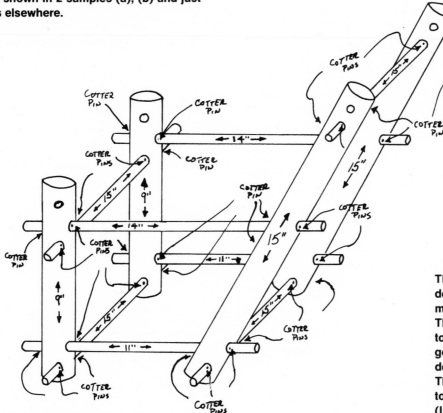

This illustrates a dry run. When you actually do the connections, you will have to put the material on the dowels (⅝″) first.

The seat material goes from 11″-long dowel to 11″-long dowel. The arm/seat material goes on a 14″-long dowel, under the 11″-long dowels, and up onto the other 14″-long dowel. The back material goes from 15″-long dowel to 15″-long dowel in back.

(I think I would probably assemble the swing temporarily, then put the material around the dowel, pinning it in position before sewing.)

MAKE YOUR OWN BABY FURNITURE

SWING FRAME

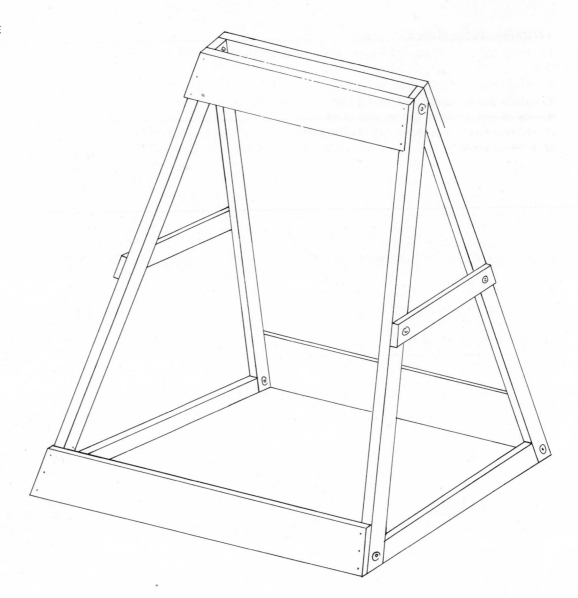

SWING FRAME—PROCEDURE

1. From the 2″ x 4″ cut six lengths of 6′ (or buy 6′ lengths), and two lengths of 38″.

2. From the 1″ x 8″ cut two lengths of 36″ and two lengths of 54″.

3. Mark two 6′ lengths (a), two lengths (b), two lengths (c).

4. As shown in illustrations, p. 130 measure for cutting out the laps on (a) and (c). Either measure a 60° angle, or use the 4″ to 6″ measurement to yield an angle close enough. Saw across the angled line down halfway deep and stop. Use a chisel to remove the wood, as shown in the chapter "Construction Techniques."

5. Measure for the laps on (b) pieces. The laps are on opposite sides of the ends, but the procedure is the same as in step 4.

6. Measure for the bolt holes on all ends and drill the holes ½″ or 9/16″ diameter.

7. Bolt the two side frames together.

8. Measure for the 1″ holes for the swing rope on the 1″ x 8″ 54″ pieces and drill holes.

9. Nail the 1″ x 8″ pieces in position for ease of working on them, but don't hammer the nails all the way in. One nail at each corner will do.

10. Predrill for three screws at each end, and screw the boards on, removing the nail as you do each end.

11. Hang the swing from the two holes in the top boards at a height convenient to you.

SWING FRAME—MATERIALS

MAKE YOUR OWN BABY FURNITURE

2″ x 4″ (1½″ x 3½″).

6'

3½″

(6)

38″

(2)

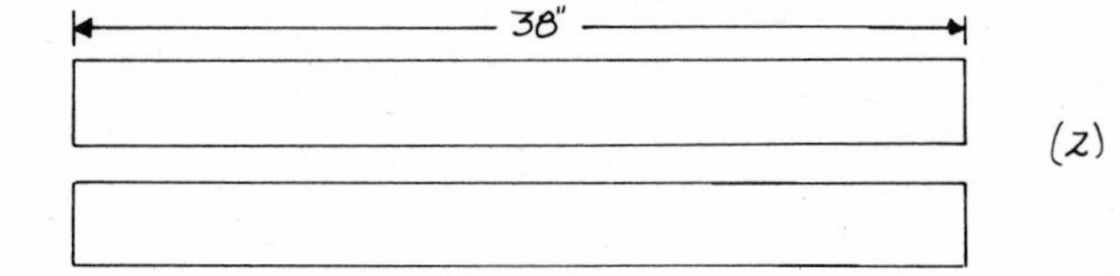

10 2″ bolts with nuts and lock washers.
1½″ #8 flathead screws.

1″ x 8″ (¾″ x 7½″).

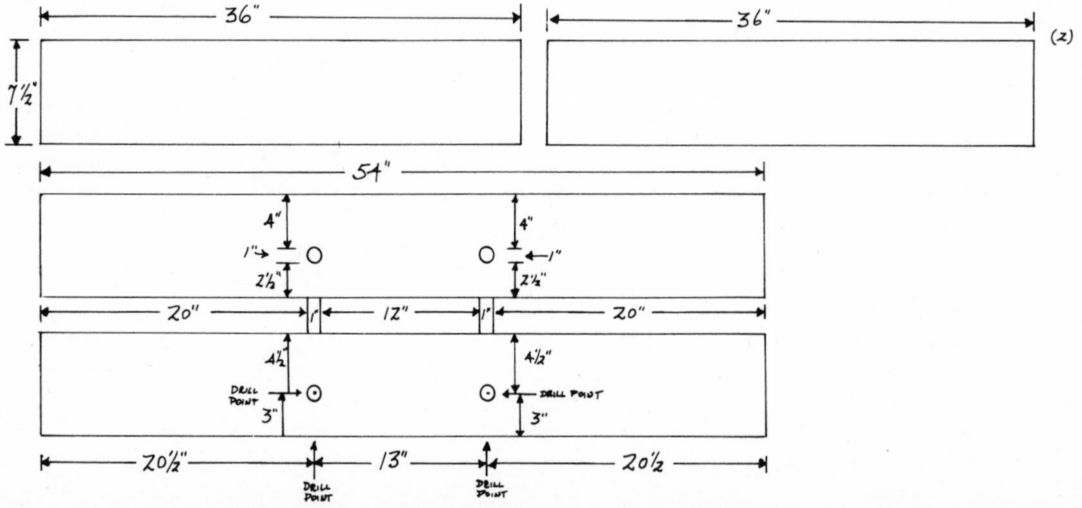

36″   36″   (2)

7½″

54″

Measurements for drill points (1″ holes for swing rope).

4″   4″
1″   1″
2½″   2½″

20″   1″   12″   1″   20″

4½″   4½″
DRILL POINT   DRILL POINT
3″   3″

20½″   13″   20½

DRILL POINT   DRILL POINT

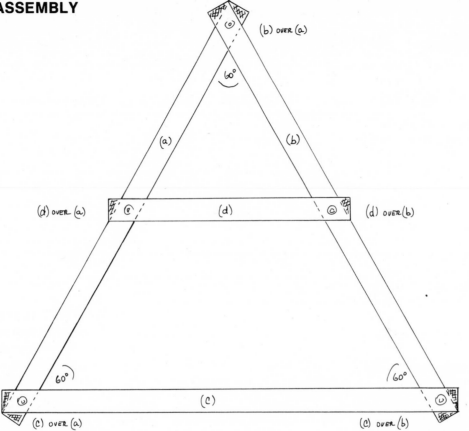

The sides of the frame will fit together as shown. The joints will be lap joints for the three corners of the triangle. (The protruding corners will be cut off.)

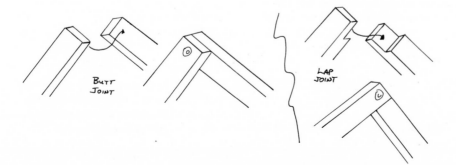

The cross-piece (d) will be butt-jointed, laid on top of (a) and (b), and bolted.

MAKE YOUR OWN BABY FURNITURE

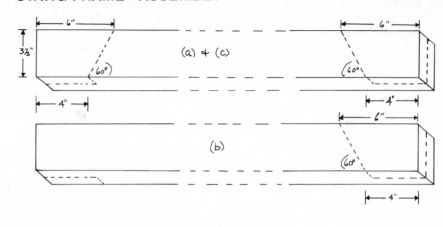

Measure for cutting out laps as shown. (a) and (c) have laps on same side. (b) has one up and down.

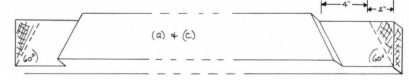

Use chisel and hammer to remove lap notch (see "Construction Techniques.").

Then measure the 60° angle and cut off edge angles.

Finally, measure for the center and drill for bolts (use ½" or 9/16" bore bit for ½" bolts).

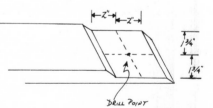

For brace (d) only, the corner angles need be cut off and the bolt hole drilled.

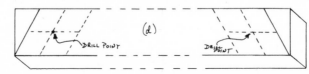

In (a) and (b) the drill point for the bolts connecting to the brace (d) are centered, 36" from each end.

SWING FRAME—ASSEMBLY

Predrill and screw the 1″ x 8″ bracing on (you may need help holding it).
Use 1½″ #8 flathead screws.

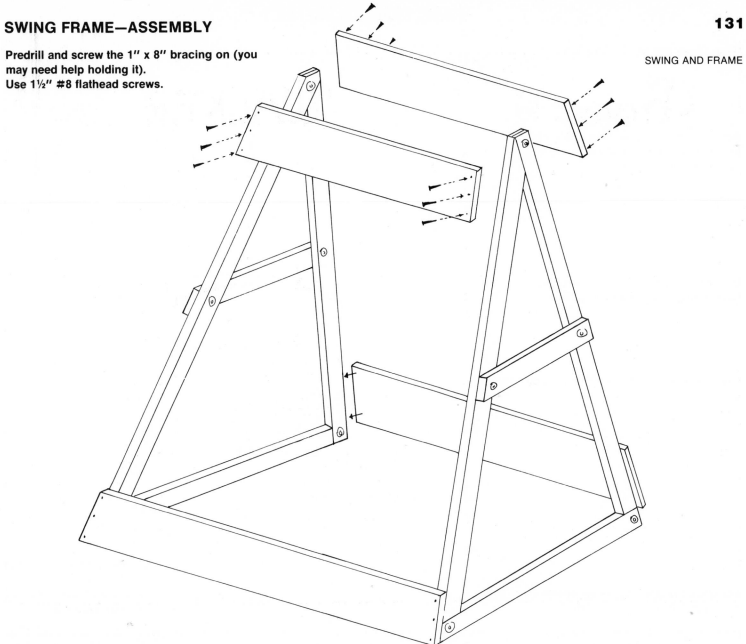

Project 9

WALKER

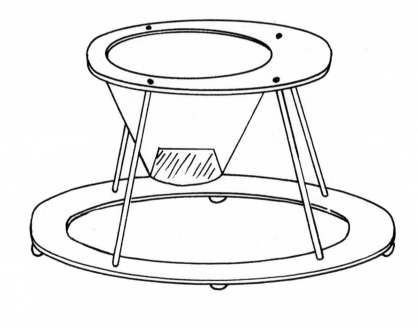

𝒯 his may well be the toy you will hate, as you watch your hardy child propel it forward into all the furniture—bang, crash. It is a gadget designed to strengthen your child's legs for walking, and I guess it works.

It certainly was a hard thing for me to design, for I had to deal with creating a structure that was strong and yet would leave foot space at the bottom. And should I or shouldn't I put a tray on it like the flimsy metal ones that are available? Should the seat be canvas or hardwood? Indecision! I guess if the choice were mine now, I would go out and buy one of those flimsies. No, wait a minute, Florence. Do a lightweight wooden frame with a canvas seat. Why not do it all! OK. OK. But no tray. They never sit still for a minute in one of these. And no beads to break off and eat. Just a plain old walker.

WALKER—PROCEDURE

1. Find an old 36″ wooden ruler, or use a 3′ length of 1″ x 3″ and make yourself a compass as shown in illustrations, p. 136. Be sure the point of your pencil will just fit through the pencil holes enough to draw onto the wood underneath. Use a countersink bit and stop when it comes through—do the drilling slowly. For the center point nail hole, make a hole only as thick as the nail, so the position of it will be secure.

2. Measure to find the center point on a ¾″ piece of plywood 28″ x 28″, by dividing it into four 14″ x 14″ squares and draw the dividing lines, as in illustration, AB and CD.

3. Puncture the center point (C1) with an awl so the compass point will go in exactly at the center. (This point will be used for the 12″ circle and the 9″ circle.)

4. Measure up 1″ from the center point on line CD and puncture another point (C2). (This will be the center point for the 5″ circle.)

5. Scribe the circle of 12″ radius from center point C1.
Scribe the circle of 9″ radius from center point C1.
Scribe the circle of 5″ radius from center point C2.

6. With a protractor, divide the 12″ circle into 45° segments, as shown in illustration, and draw lines EF and GH.

WALKER

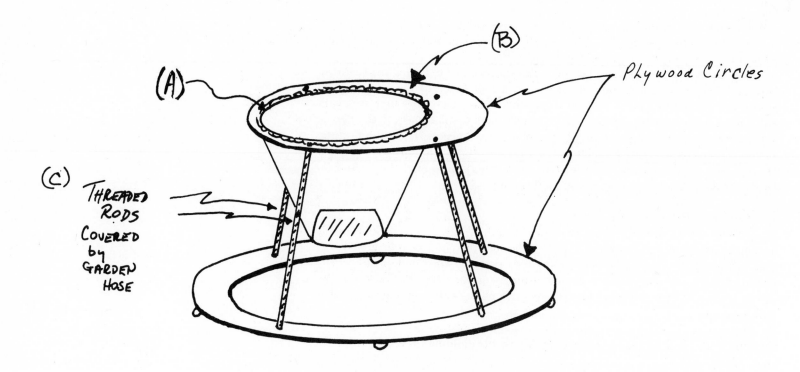

Plywood Circles

(A)

(B)

(C) THREADED RODS COVERED by GARDEN HOSE

(a) Seat stapled to upper side of top circle.
(b) Top circle should then be covered with padded material.
(c) Threaded rods (between upper and lower circles) should be covered with lengths of garden hose slipped over rods.

7. Between the 12″ and 9″ circles, measure for centered drill points along lines EF and GH.

Between the 9″ circle and the 5″ circle measure for centered drill points also on lines EF and GH.

Puncture the drill points with an awl.

8. Drill ⅜″ holes in the outer ring (between the 12″ and 9″ circles) at an angle inward toward the center, aiming, for example, from G toward H, etc.*

9. Drill ⅜″ holes in the inner ring (between the 9″ and 5″ circles) at an angle outward, away from the center, aiming, for example, from the center toward G, etc.*

10. On the outer ring, between the 12″ and 9″ circles, mark X points along lines AB and CD for the placement of the wheels.

11. Drill a hole big enough for a saw blade on the inside of the 5″ circle and cut out the inner circle.

12. Drill a hole for the saw blade through the 9″ line and cut out the second circle.

13. Drill a hole for the saw blade on the outside of the 12″ circle and cut out that circle.

14. Slip the threaded rods through, placing washer, lock washer, and nut on both sides of the wood, and tighten. The lock washers act as a spring to keep the nut from unscrewing.

15. Cut out the material for the seat, baste, and sew.

16. Staple the seat in position to the upper ring.

17. The upper ring could then be covered with some padded material and so could the lower ring, to prevent furniture damage.

---

* If you look at the illustration, you will see that the threaded rods will go through the rings at an angle, inward and upward from the bottom ring toward the top ring.

MAKE YOUR OWN BABY FURNITURE

¾" plywood (A-D) (use 28" x 28" to give yourself room).

Compass:

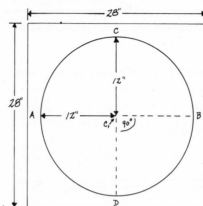

1) Draw the large circle (12" radius) first. (Center at C1.) Also draw guidelines AB and CD which are perpendicular.

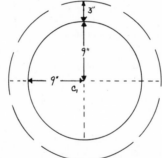

2) Next, using the same center point (C1), draw the second circle (9" radius).
Make a compass out of a thin strip of wood or a long wooden ruler.
Drill a thin hole for a nail and three larger holes for pencil point to fit through.
(Countersink the start of the hole after drilling through for pencil point.)

Make a compass out of a thin strip of wood or a long wooden ruler.

3) Move the center point (C2) up 1" from C1 and draw the third circle, (5" radius).

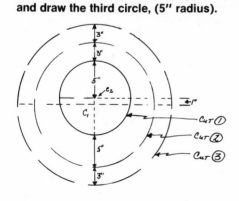

4) Further divide into 45° segments. Drawing lines EF and GH. Mark drill points for threaded rods. (Points are in 1" from outer edge.)

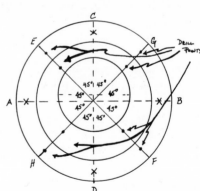

5) Cut out third circle (5") first, second circle (9") next, first circle (12") last.
6) Wheels will go on at "x" points.

See next page about drilling angle.

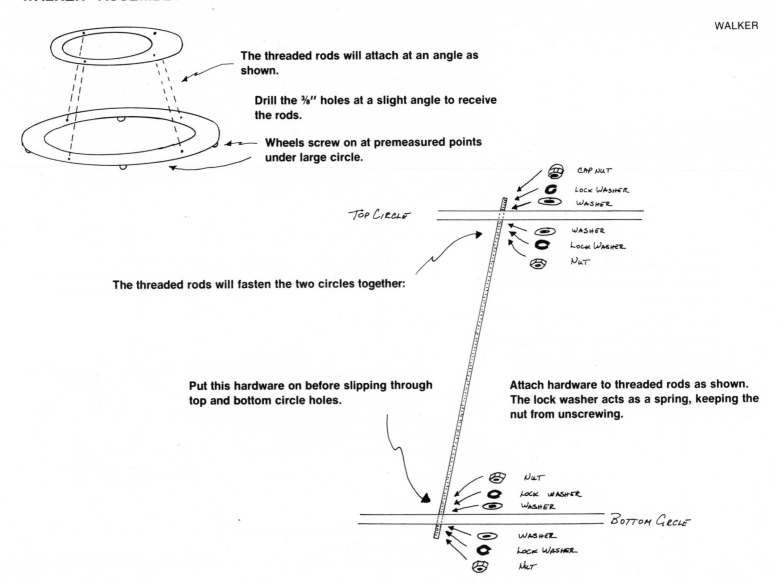

The threaded rods will attach at an angle as shown.

Drill the ⅜" holes at a slight angle to receive the rods.

Wheels screw on at premeasured points under large circle.

The threaded rods will fasten the two circles together:

Put this hardware on before slipping through top and bottom circle holes.

Attach hardware to threaded rods as shown. The lock washer acts as a spring, keeping the nut from unscrewing.

CAP NUT
LOCK WASHER
WASHER

TOP CIRCLE

WASHER
LOCK WASHER
NUT

NUT
LOCK WASHER
WASHER

BOTTOM CIRCLE

WASHER
LOCK WASHER
NUT

MAKE YOUR OWN BABY FURNITURE

WALKER—CANVAS SEAT

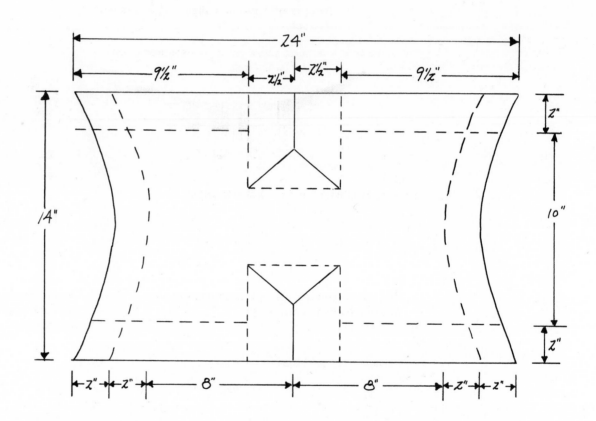

**Cut on solid lines; fold on dotted lines; fold
on dotted lines and seam (double).**

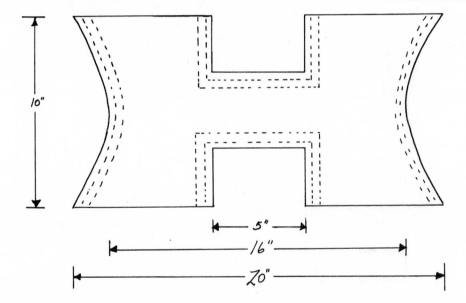

Project 10

Toys

𝒯his will be the most fun! and making a toy is just one more way to give you and your child time, either together or by yourselves, according to the "toy-babysitter" premise. The more complicated and exciting and challenging the toy, the more time. You may not appreciate my seemingly cynical attitude yet, if you are just starting your family, but any normal family will eventually bring you to some similar reactions—days when you want to fill a kerchief with some bread and cheese and run away from home! The mixed emotions of loving your kids fully and wonderfully . . . and wondering if you can live with them another day.

You know, the most wonderful thing about wooden toys is their durability. A kid could throw one out a fourth-story window and the most that would probably happen is that it would need some more glue. In fact, you'll soon know, if you don't already, the frustration of trying to fix a beloved but broken plastic toy. YUK! Besides, you have made the toy, so you know how it goes together. Pie of a fix. At worst, if it is truly beyond repair, you can make another!

It would be fun to fill a book with toys you might make. But you will notice, after you have made some of these, that your eye will stray here and there, to toy ads or toys in stores, and you will begin to feel the nudge inside you. At first an unsure whisper, but then stronger. "I bet I could make one of those." And you will. Neat, huh?

There's a future bonus that comes with all this building. Your children will watch . . . and learn. My children have built three tree houses and one underground house since we moved here four years ago, and two go-carts, and one "camper" three stories high! I watched them push and pull it down the road . . . and then stood and sadly watched them pick up the pieces after it fell over. Yes, they do their own toys now. David had duplicated all the *Star Wars* guns and ships within days of seeing the movie. It's great. But boy, do they wreck my tools. Misplace them . . . always. That's OK. I have finally come to a resolution about that. This Christmas they will get their own tools, and mine will be locked up. I don't care what they lose. They're not getting momma's tools anymore! So . . . plan ahead. While you're saving up for their college, put a few bucks aside for their tool kits.

Save scrap wood—you'll find hundreds of uses for it in toys. If you have a woodworking shop nearby, raid their garbage bins at night. You'll find fantastic goodies in all shapes and sizes, as well as some good hardwoods. Let your imagination flow. (And if you have a wood-burning stove, the scraps found in the dumper will also be good kindling.)

Toys, like the furniture, will be chewed on and eaten by your teether, so use nontoxic paint and a spray vinyl covering.

Finally, there is a large bonus once you have created some of these playthings. You will be able to make presents for others. Or you could even go into business. Think on that for a while. Enjoy . . . you just walked into toyland!

About the toys included . . .

Some of my son Sam's favorite toys were puzzles, at first the kind with only five or six pieces. Then as he grew, he needed more complicated puzzles. I remember he had fifteen or twenty of those starter puzzles, and I bought shelves to store them in—because I didn't have my "hammering head" yet. Your child can have as many of these puzzles as you can invent themes. The themes I suggest here, shapes, animals, fruit, are just the beginning. You can trace drawings from children's books, dictionaries, encyclopedias, comics, etc.

Blocks are also a forever favorite. They are expensive when you get into quantity, but so easy to make yourself. You could start now, doing a few pieces a week, cutting and sanding, and even as your child plays with them, the block collection can grow.

Another favorite toy is people. A box full of people and their environments— house, farm, firehouse, trucks, cars—become an afternoon's fantasy. The dowel people are easy to make. A short length of thick dowel with heads carved at the top. Their identity is painted on: woman, man, child, firefighter, doctor, monster, whatever. A slab of wood with wheels carved and holes drilled for the people to sit in becomes a vehicle. Environments are also easy. Small boxes, like the cube, become houses, farms, schoolrooms, firehouses. Variations on the people carvings will produce animals or even robots. Yes, there's no end to this wonderful toy. I have also included a rocker that will grow into a vehicle when your child can handle it. They have the same frame with removable sides. One day the rocker can be an elephant, the next it can be a swan. When your child is more mobile, the rocker sides can be discarded (to the scrap wood pile for some other future) and vehicle sides attached at the same time that wheels are added. Again, there can be a variety of sides available to add some versatility. No kid wants to drive an ice cream truck all the time. There are days for the fire engine . . . or the ship cruise . . . or the space flight.

You can have fun with the vehicle, finding gadgets to add. Horns—no, you don't want a horn!—lights that hook on, bike lights maybe . . . a small wagon that attaches behind and gives rides to all the stuffed animals . . . or a back seat for a friend.

The seesaw was a last-minute idea I had. On a rainy day when you can't get to the park, and invite a small friend over to play, this toy will provide an alternative after the little people and puzzles are worn out. Be sure to pad the undersides of the ends with some thick carpeting remnants to protect your floor—and your ears—from the thumping fun of the excited children banging up and down. Maybe you'll want this to be one of the outdoor toys.

The easel is one that will sit on a table, rather than one of those tall, spindly, tippable kinds. I opt for this because if the standing one goes over, so goes the paint; and this style folds up and tucks away in some corner, freeing space.

Finally, the gadget board. Surely you will have ten more ideas to add to this or additional boards. I remember the children's as one we related to together. "Where is red?" That sort of thing.

A word of caution about toys for the toddler. Everything goes in the mouth. Make nothing that is swallowable–choke-on-able. Always check the toys for loose parts and hardware as a matter of habit. Try to refrain from buying things like cars with tiny wheels that can come off. (That was my choking baby experience.) Merry every day to your Imogene!

MAKE YOUR OWN BABY FURNITURE

ROCKER/VEHICLE

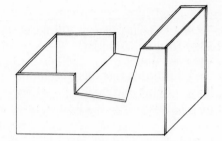

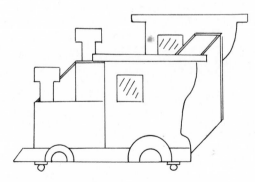

ROCKER/VEHICLE—PROCEDURE

1. From the 1″ x 12″ board, one at a time, measure for and cut out back, seat back, front, rocker footrest, and seat.

2. From the plywood measure for and cut out the sides.

3. From the 2″ x 4″ cut out two lengths of 13″.

4. From the 1″ x 1″ cut out one length of 13″.

5. Use corner clamps and glue the back and front between the sides.

6. Predrill for screws and screw the four parts together.

7. Glue the seat back in position and predrill and screw it into position.

8. Lay the seat on the sides, glue, predrill, and nail the seat onto the sides.

9. Predrill and screw the hand-hold bar between the sides.

10. Turn the frame upside down.

11. For the rocker, select a design and make an actual size template from the patterns. Trace it onto ½″ plywood and cut out the shape. Draw the features, paint it, whatever, and bolt it onto the sides of the frame. Use five nuts/bolts/ washers: two, upper and lower, at back; two, upper and lower, at front; and one under the seat section, placed according to your design. Use ⅜″ bolts, 2″ long, and predrill for them once the locations are decided.

12. When the time comes to modify this into a vehicle, glue and nail the wheel braces to the under edges of the frame. Add wheels to the wheel braces under the frame. Unbolt the rocker sides. Attach vehicle sides constructed the same way the rocker sides were made, step 11.

ROCKER/VEHICLE—MATERIALS

1″ by 12″ (¾″ by 11½″)

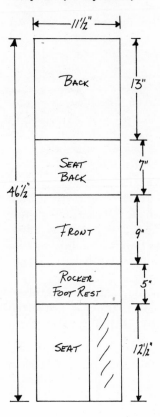

½″ plywood (A-C) (22″ x 23″).

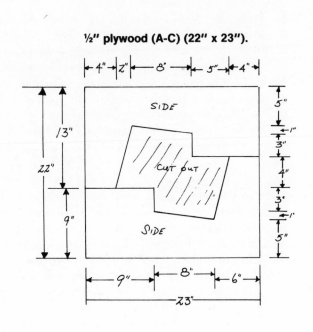

2″ x 4″ (1½″ x 3½″).

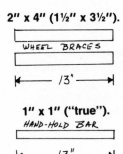

1″ x 1″ ("true").

HAND-HOLD BAR

1″ #6 flathead screws.
1¼″ common nails.
Carpenter's glue.

For vehicle: 4 wheels.

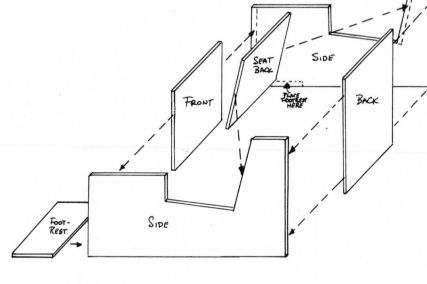

1) Glue and screw back, seat back, front and
footrest *between* sides.
(Use 1″ #6 flathead screws.)

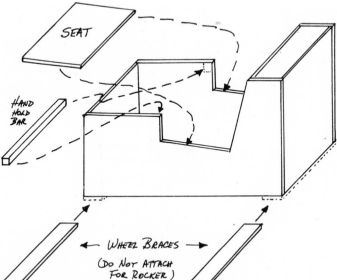

2) Glue and nail seat down onto edges of
frame. (Use 1¼″ common nails.)

3) Screw hand-hold (1″ x 1″) bar between
sides. This completes preparation for rocker.

4) Later, when changing from rocker to
vehicle, turn frame upside down and glue and
nail wheel braces to under edges of frame as
shown. (Use 1¼″ common nails.) Screw
wheels under braces at ends.

ROCKER SHAPES

MAKE YOUR OWN BABY FURNITURE

Screw to sides of frame.

= 3 SQUARE INCHS

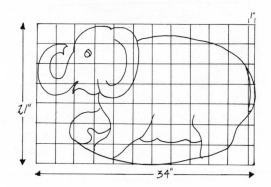

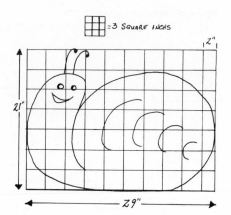

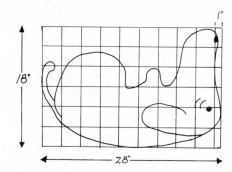

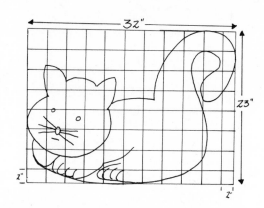

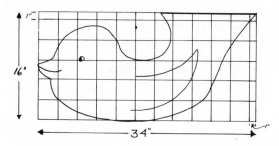

There are ducks, swans, horses, unicorns, whales, porpoises, sharks, lambs, piggies, hippopotamuses, bulls, cows, turkeys, octopuses, turtles, camels, and crocodiles.

VEHICLE SIDES

Screw to side of frame.

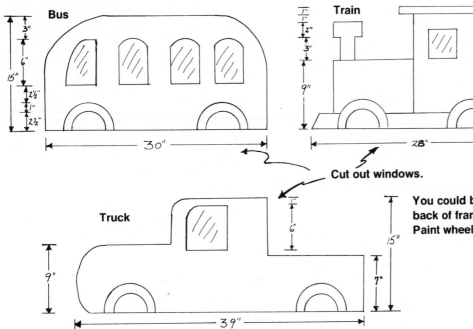

Bus

3"

6"

15"

2½"

1"

2½"

30"

Train

1"

1"

2"

3"

9"

16"

28"

Cut out windows.

Truck

1"

6"

15"

9"

7"

39"

You could build a box and nail it inside to
back of frame and to sides of truck.
Paint wheels on.

Your car (if you want).

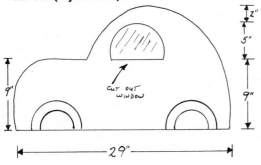

2"

5"

9"

9"

CUT OUT
WINDOW

29"

And there are Conestoga
wagons, ice cream trucks,
fire engines, airplanes,
helicopters, Zeppelins,
balloons, and spaceships!

Sailboat

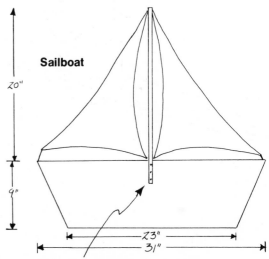

20"

9"

23"

31"

Screw a piece of 1" x 1" onto
side to hold sails made of sheet.

SEESAW

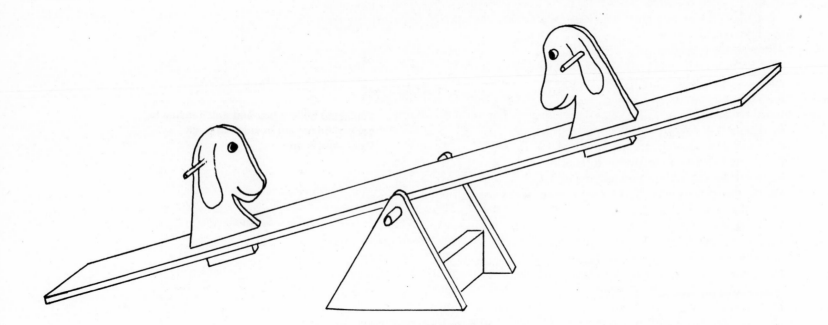

SEESAW—PROCEDURE

1. Cut a 5′ length of 1″ x 6″.

2. Measure for the head slots, drill a hole big enough for a saw blade, and cut the slots out. (You will want the slots to be tight, so cut inside the lines. Enlarge later if you have to.)

3. On the 1″ x 12″ board measure for two lengths of 10″. Then measure for the triangular cuts as shown. (Best to have a longer board to work with.) Make the triangular cuts at one end, then cut the 10″ lengths off. Do the same for the second triangle.

4. On these triangles, measure for the 1¼″-diameter dowel holes, C-clamp the triangle to a table and drill out these holes. (This could be done before the triangles are cut, which might be easier.)

5. Make an actual-size template for the dog's head and trace it onto the 1″ x 8″ board twice, as shown. Use a scroll saw blade to cut out these shapes.

6. From 2″ x 4″ cut out two lengths of 5 9/16″.

7. From 1¼″ dowel, cut one length of 10″.

8. From ¾″ dowel cut two lengths of 8″.

9. From ½″ dowel cut two lengths of 3″.

10. On the underside of the 1″ x 12″ board, screw the half-circle braces on at the edges of the center line.

11. Drill the peg holes in the heads as shown.

12. Slip the heads through the board slots and peg into place. Then predrill and screw the board to the head, as shown.

13. Construct the stand by placing the braces between the triangular sections and predrilling and screwing together.

14. Drill holes in the 1¼″ dowel for the cotter pins, as shown.

15. Hold the seat board over the stand, slip the 1¼″ dowel through the stand's holes and through the half-circle braces under the board.

16. Cotter pin the 1¼″ dowel in position.

17. You may want to nail some old rug pieces to the underside edges of the board to protect your floors and ears.

MATERIALS

1" x 6" (¾" x 5½")

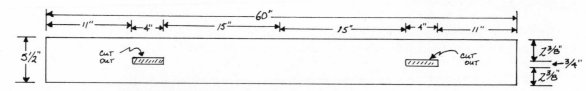

Be careful measuring: My 1" x 6" was only 5-1/16" wide, not 5½", and I had to compensate to get the hole ¾".

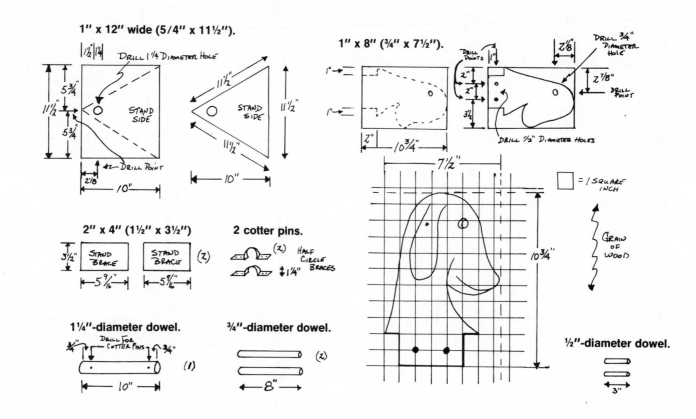

1" x 12" wide (5/4" x 11½").

DRILL 1¼ DIAMETER HOLE

STAND SIDE

STAND SIDE

#2 Drill Point

1" x 8" (¾" x 7½").

DRILL POINTS

DRILL ¾" DIAMETER HOLE

DRILL POINT

DRILL ½" DIAMETER HOLES

□ = 1 SQUARE INCH

GRAIN OF WOOD

2" x 4" (1½" x 3½")

STAND BRACE   STAND BRACE   (2)

2 cotter pins.

(2) HALF CIRCLE BRACES ↕1¼"

1¼"-diameter dowel.

DRILL FOR COTTER PINS   (1)

¾"-diameter dowel.

(2)

½"-diameter dowel.

SEESAW—ASSEMBLY

**1) Screw in half-circle braces—use ½"
flathead screws.**

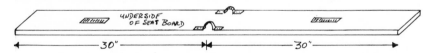

**2) * See note below.
Glue inside hole; push ¾" dowel through.**

**3) Slip head end through slot,
glue holes underneath, and
push ½" pegs through.**

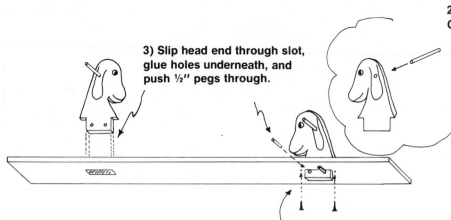

**4) Screw up through board into edge of head
resting on board (½" away from slot).
(Use 1¼" #8 flathead screws.)
(Actually, if you want a nice snug dowel fit
under the head, drill the holes slightly higher
and then shave the dowels a bit flat where
they will meet the board—only on one end of
the dowel, the end you will push in.)**

5) Screw stand sides to supports.

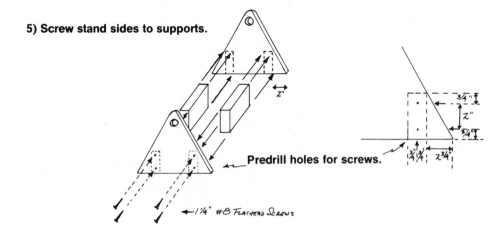

Predrill holes for screws.

*** *Note:* Sometimes holes drilled with a bore
bit the same size as the dowel diameter are
too large for the dowel. Use a bore bit 1/16"
smaller. Also, if dowel is still wiggly, cut some
thin shavings of wood and force into spaces.
These, plus glue, should hold dowels.**

MAKE YOUR OWN BABY FURNITURE

SEESAW—ASSEMBLY

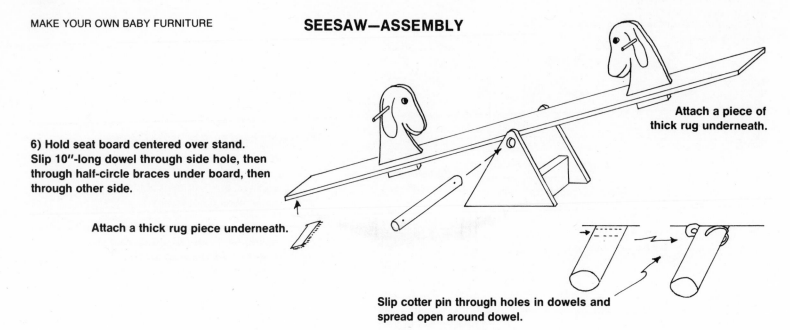

6) Hold seat board centered over stand. Slip 10"-long dowel through side hole, then through half-circle braces under board, then through other side.

Attach a piece of thick rug underneath.

Attach a thick rug piece underneath.

Slip cotter pin through holes in dowels and spread open around dowel.

BUILDING BLOCKS—PROCEDURE

1. Cut as many of each shape as you wish; sand. 2" x 4" isn't always exactly 1½" x 3½", so measure what you get. The rectangle shape should be twice as long as the width. The square should be square, etc. Use the measurement of the width as your measurement, instead of 3½".

2. Cut as many 2"-diameter dowel sections as you wish and sand, again being guided by the width of the 2" x 4".

3. If you make a few roof sections from the 2" x 4", cut enough ¼" x ¼" lattice to make a few roofs, because these may break.

4. Play with the blocks as you make them and you'll get an idea about the quantity you will want.

TOYS—BUILDING BLOCKS

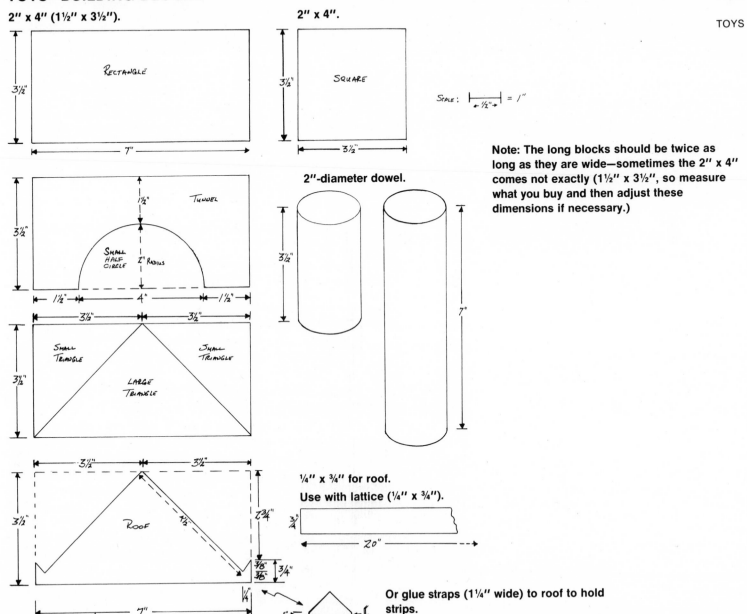

2″ x 4″ (1½″ x 3½″).

Rectangle

3½″

7″

2″ x 4″.

Square

3½″

3½″

Scale: ├──── ½″ → ┤ = 1″

Tunnel

Small Half Circle   2″ Radius

1½″   4″   1½″

3½″   1½″

2″-diameter dowel.

3½″

3½″   3½″

Small Triangle   Small Triangle

Large Triangle

3½″

7″

Note: The long blocks should be twice as long as they are wide—sometimes the 2″ x 4″ comes not exactly (1½″ x 3½″, so measure what you buy and then adjust these dimensions if necessary.)

3½″   3½″

Roof   4½″   2¾″

3½″   ⅜″   ⅜″   ¾″

7″   ¼″

¼″ x ¾″ for roof.

Use with lattice (¼″ x ¾″).

¾″

20″

Or glue straps (1¼″ wide) to roof to hold strips.

1″   7″

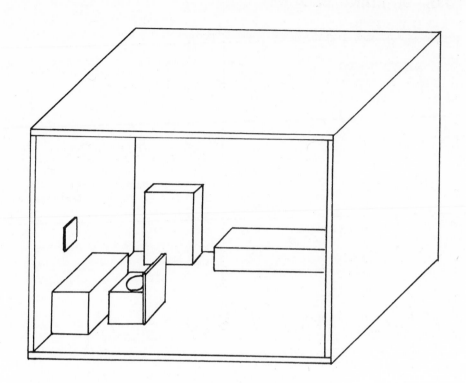

PEOPLE AND ENVIRONMENTS—PROCEDURE

1. Cut as many 3″ lengths of 1¼″ dowel as you want people.

2. Place each 3″ length of dowel in a table vise and saw around, in about ⅛″ for a guide to the carving.

3. The heads, of course, don't have to be exactly round. You could sand the top to give the curve and just carve the neck. X-acto tools are excellent for this kind of carving—be careful.

4. Environments are simply cubes or rectangular boxes like the initial cube you made.

5. Vehicles are lengths of 2″ x 4″ with short lengths of 1″ x 4″ shaped as sides with wheels (see illus.) screwed into them . . . no moving wheels to come off and choke a child at the early ages.

People—actual size: 1¼″-diameter dowel, 3″ people.

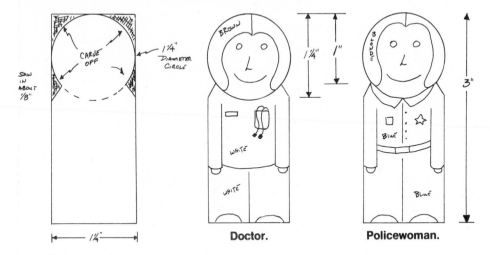

Doctor.

Policewoman.

Environments can most easily be created from cubes or rectangles.

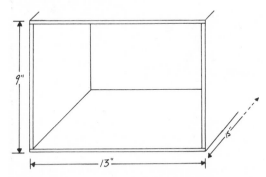

Vehicles can be made from blocks of 2″ x 4″ with 1½″ holes drilled through for people to sit in.

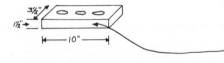

Furnishings for the environments can be constructed from leftover scrap wood.
This is a toy that will be played with. Best not to use nails or screws that might come loose and get eaten. Carpenter's glue will hold pieces together for a long time.

Rather than risk small wheels and nails coming loose, I would just glue vehicle sides to 2″ x 4″ basic vehicle (and reglue when it comes off, if it does.) Or maybe use screw nails, which are extremely hard to get out. A screw nail is a flathead like a nail with circular thread; you hammer it in.

GADGET BOARD FOR SIDE OF PLAYPEN

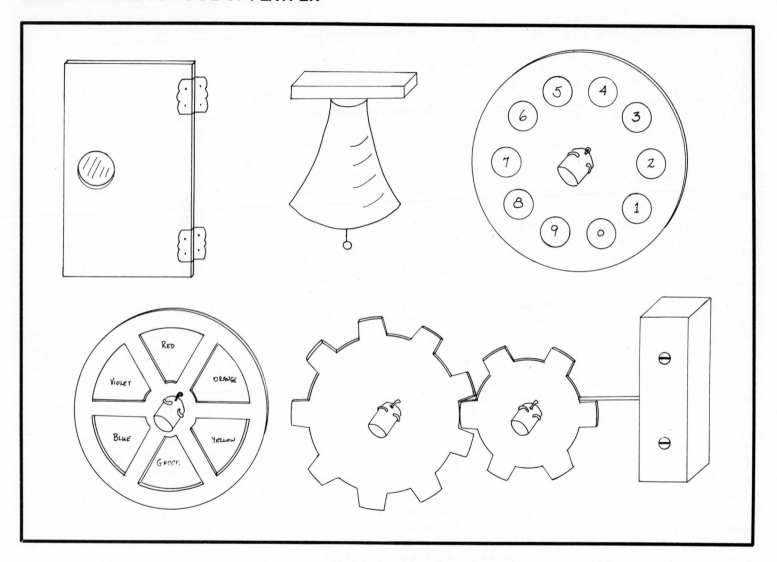

GADGET BOARD—PROCEDURE

Probably the best way to approach this project is to draw all the shapes on the plywood first, then cut out and drill the small inner sections first.

1. Scribe three 3″-diameter circles on a piece of ¼″ plywood, and one 2″-diameter circle.

Draw a 2″ x 3¼″ rectangle on the plywood also.

2. On the rectangle measure for the ½″ finger hole in the door as shown, and drill the hole out.

3. On the color wheel circle measure six inner 60° segments and cut out. Drill out the center hole of ⅜″ diameter.

4. On the telephone dial circle, measure for the ten finger holes and the center hole, and drill out.

5. On the remaining two circles—the gear circles—draw the gear layout. (Perhaps it would be best to prepare a template for each of these ahead of time and trace them on.) Cut out the center hole of ⅜″ in each.

6. Cut out the door and each of the circles, except the gears. Cut these out to design, using a scroll saw blade.

7. Paint each of the pieces.

8. Prepare to cut out the noisemaker brace of 2″ x 4″ end by first measuring for the screw holes and drilling them out. Then saw the end off. Place the end in a table vise so that you may hold the saw vertically and saw only halfway through or less. Cut a piece of plastic, sand it so it has no rough edges. Cut it to fit in the slot of the 2″ x 4″ end.

9. On the backboard, measure for the rectangular mirror, cut the mirror out of some Mylar, and glue it on.

10. Measure for and drill ⅜″ holes to hold the gears and the telephone dial. Measure for the placement of the noisemaker and then for the screw spots to hold it on. Puncture the screw points with an awl. (Don't predrill. Here the wood won't split.)

11. Paint the backboard.

12. On a length of ⅜″ dowel, measure off four 1½″ pieces. (Don't cut them yet.) Measure for the cotter pin holes in each, as shown, and put the dowel in a table vise and drill the cotter pin holes. Then you can cut the dowels into 1½″ pieces.

13. Attach the four circles by inserting a dowel plug through the circle and the backboard and securing with a cotter pin on each side. I would suggest that you then wrap some masking tape around the front protruding dowel, covering the cotter pin points, which, though not sharp, might hurt the baby . . . and check the tape periodically.

14. Hinge the door in position.

15. Screw the noisemaker, with plastic, in position.

MAKE YOUR OWN BABY FURNITURE

GADGET BOARD—ASSEMBLY

Cut-outs from ¼″ plywood.

Door (hinge to backboard).

Telephone dial.

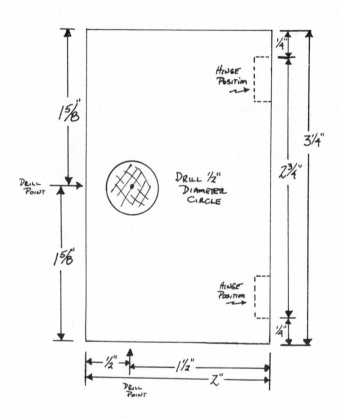

Paste Mylar (same size as door) on
backboard behind door.

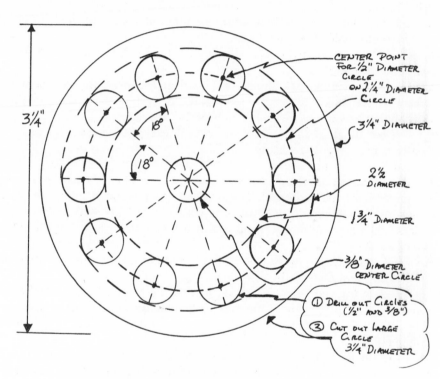

Measure 18° segments; mark center point on
1⅛″ circle for ½″ circles.
Lay circle on backboard and paint on
numbers 0–9 on backboard. If you also paint
numbers on the dial near the circle, the task
will be more challenging.

Color wheel.

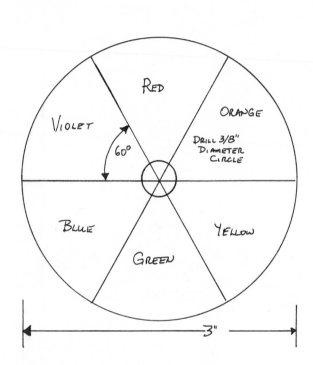

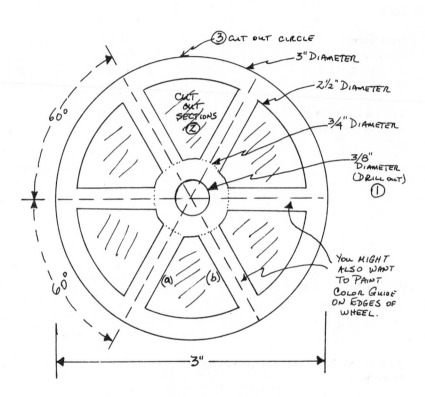

On backboard, draw 3″-diameter circle, measure 60° segments. Paint the sections. Drill the center hole—⅜″ diameter.

On separate ¼″ plywood prepare to cut the color wheel; measure for circles, draw segment lines (a) (b) ⅛″ away from 60° segment lines. Cut out 6 segments and center ⅜″ circle.

MAKE YOUR OWN BABY FURNITURE

Gears.

Draw circles.
Measure segments:
20° on large gear.
30° on small gear.

It is necessary to square the gear off so it will fit in the corresponding space of the other gear.

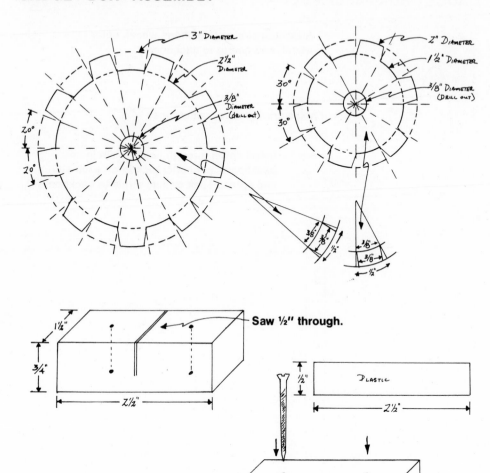

Noisemaker. **(Cut a ¾″ piece of a 2″ x 4″ end.)**

Obtain a hard, thin piece of plastic for noisemaker.

Screw to backboard (1¼″ #8 flathead screws).

Glue slit; Insert plastic in slit and screw to backboard.

Let 1¼″ protrude.

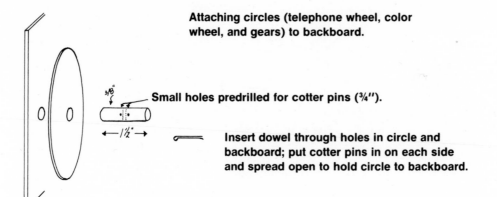

Attaching circles (telephone wheel, color wheel, and gears) to backboard.

Small holes predrilled for cotter pins (¾").

Insert dowel through holes in circle and backboard; put cotter pins in on each side and spread open to hold circle to backboard.

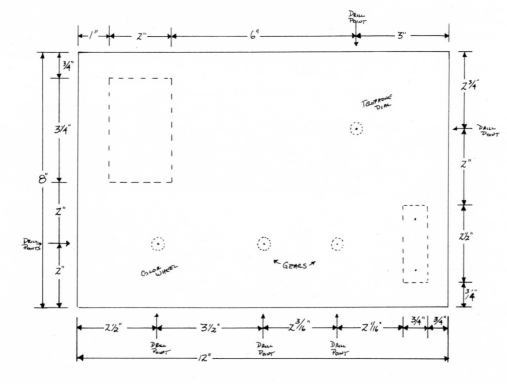

Backboard positioning.

PUZZLES—PROCEDURE

1. From ¼" plywood cut as many 8" x 12" rectangles as you want puzzles.

2. From ⅛" Masonite also cut as many 8" x 12" rectangles as you want puzzles.

3. Draw the shapes on the Masonite front piece.

4. Although I have suggested three techniques for cutting out the shapes, two of which yield the puzzle pieces at the same time, I do believe that the easiest method will be to cut the shapes out of the front board without attempting to get the puzzle pieces at the same time. Cut the pieces from another piece of Masonite. At least this was true for me when I tried to do the job. The job is immensely easier with this method. So . . . cut the shapes from the front board. Cut the puzzle pieces from another. Glue the front board (Masonite) to the backboard (plywood), paint it and the puzzle pieces—and go on to the next puzzle.

Note: My puzzles are rather primitive, basic themes. There are hundreds of other choices . . . ice cream cones, pumpkins, watermelons, telephones, vehicles, animals, hearts, flowers, hats, tools; and books, dictionaries, newspapers and magazines full of endless ideas.

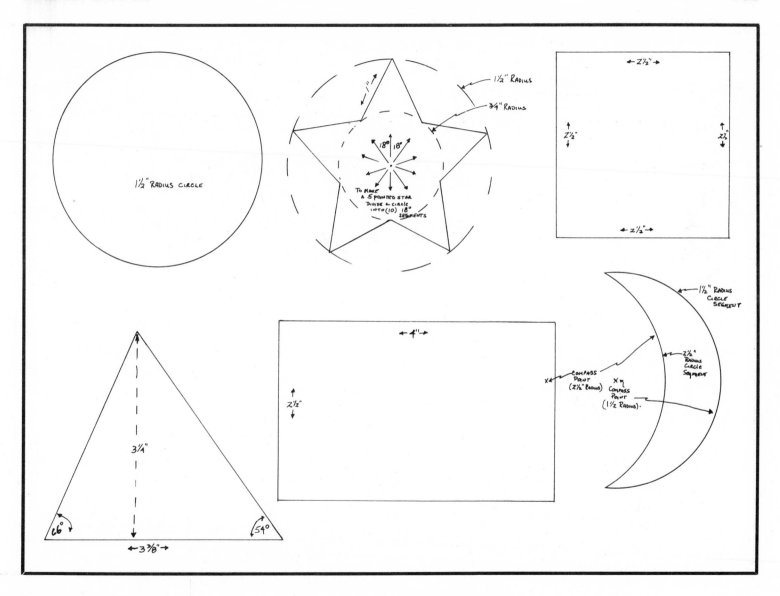

166

PUZZLE: FLYING THINGS

MAKE YOUR OWN BABY FURNITURE

¼″ plywood (A-D).

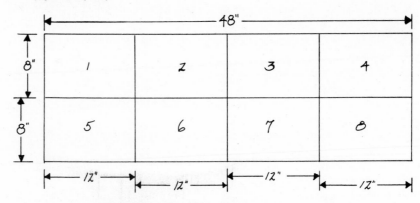

Top section of puzzles, from which to cut shapes.
Cut *through* the lines you draw.

⅛″ Masonite.

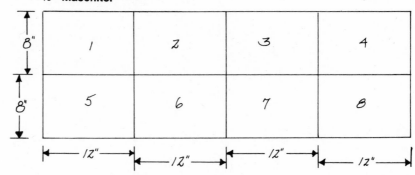

Use for puzzle backing.
After shapes cut out of plywood, leave shapes aside and glue plywood 8″ x 12″ to rough side of Masonite 8″ x 12″.

Use a "scrolling" saw blade in your saw.
(a) Drill a hole first with a bit that has a diameter a little larger than saw-blade width. Center it along some line, as opposed to at a corner. Cut slowly and round square corners.
(b) Another option is to cut through from one shape to another. (If you have access to a band saw, this would be best for cutting out the shapes.)
(c) Another option is to cut the shapes out anyway you can and cut the puzzle pieces from another piece of Masonite.

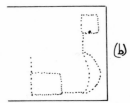

PUZZLE SHELVES—PROCEDURE

1. From a piece of ½″ plywood, or remnants from other projects, measure for and cut out the top, bottom, sides, and back.

2. From the parting bead, measure for and cut, one at a time, fourteen lengths of 9″.

3. Measure for the placement of the cleats on the insides of the sides and glue and nail the cleats in position.

4. Glue and corner-clamp the sides between the top and bottom and nail the box together.

5. Turn the box on its front edges and glue and nail the back to the back edges of the box.

6. Paint if you wish.

PUZZLE SHELVES

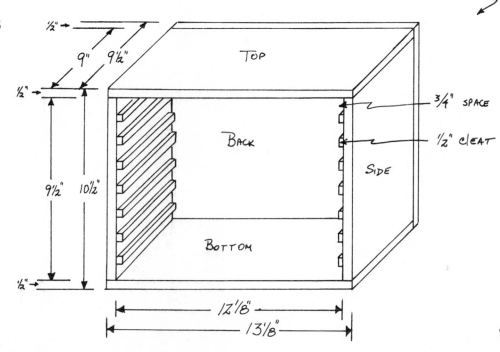

☐ = 1 SQUARE INCH

Will hold 8 puzzles.

PUZZLE SHELVES—MATERIALS

½" plywood (A-D).

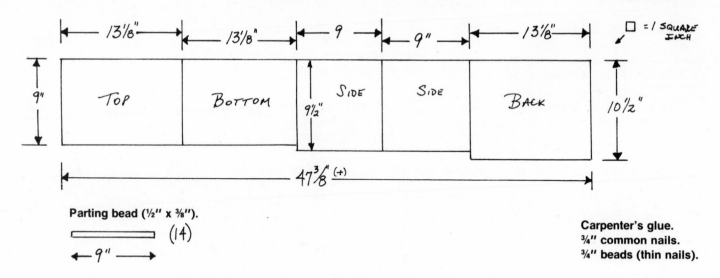

□ = 1 SQUARE INCH

Parting bead (½" x ⅜"). (14)

← 9" →

Carpenter's glue.
¾" common nails.
¾" beads (thin nails).

PUZZLE SHELVES—ASSEMBLY

Measure and draw lines on *sides* (tops of cleats will meet lines).

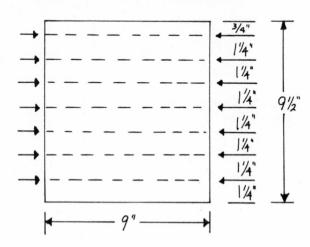

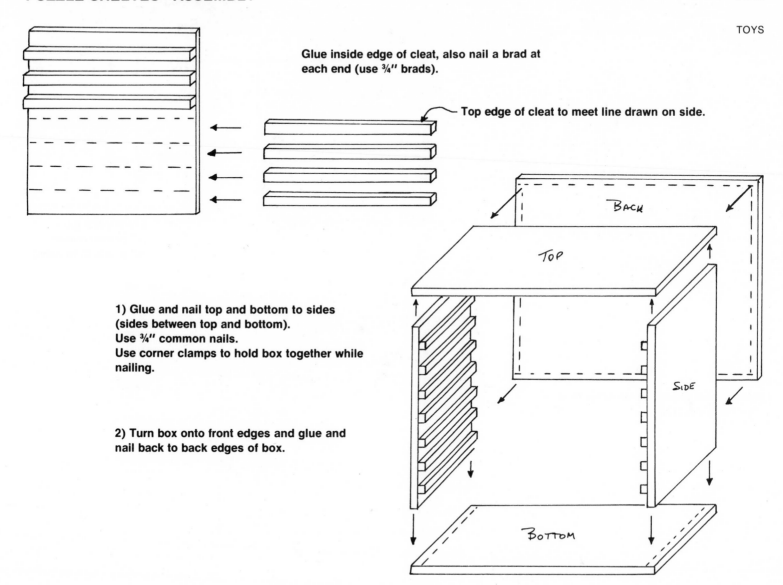

Glue inside edge of cleat, also nail a brad at each end (use ¾″ brads).

Top edge of cleat to meet line drawn on side.

1) Glue and nail top and bottom to sides (sides between top and bottom).
Use ¾″ common nails.
Use corner clamps to hold box together while nailing.

2) Turn box onto front edges and glue and nail back to back edges of box.

BACK

TOP

SIDE

BOTTOM

MAKE YOUR OWN BABY FURNITURE

EASEL/BLACKBOARD—PROCEDURE

1. Measure for and cut three pieces for the easel/blackboard. Two, for the front and back, should be the same size. The third, for the bottom piece, may be narrower.

2. If you want one side, or both, to function as a blackboard, there is "blackboard" paint available to use.

3. Hinge the front to the back and the front to the bottom.

4. Attach hook and eye lock from the inside of the back to the inside of the bottom—when unlatched the unit can be folded and tucked away.

5. Two or four large clips will hold paper for drawing, finger painting, etc. in place.

6. Make this unit of a size that will fit on one of the little tables following, leaving room for paint jars and crayons, etc. beside the easel.

EASEL/BLACKBOARD

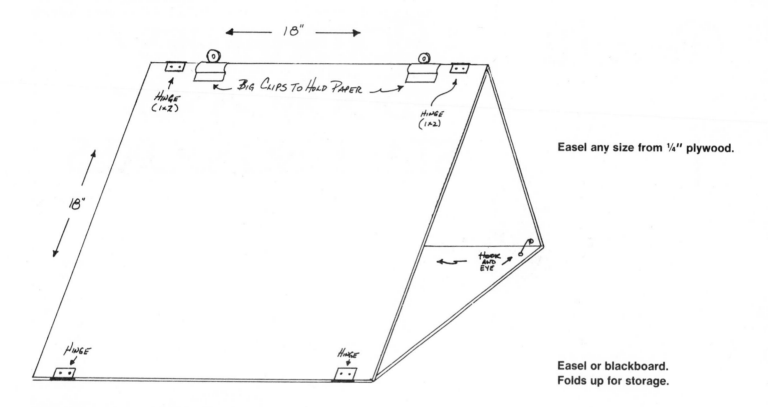

18"

18"

HINGE
(1×2)

BIG CLIPS TO HOLD PAPER

HINGE
(1×2)

HOOK
AND
EYE

HINGE

HINGE

Easel any size from ¼" plywood.

Easel or blackboard.
Folds up for storage.

This can be used on a table. I like this style
better than the flimsy standing kind, which
kick over easily. (Paint all over the floor is
what that means!)
Blackboard: There is a paint called
blackboard paint that some say is adequate.
I think I would scrounge around thrift shops
and dumps for a genuine slate blackboard.

176

Project 11

Toy Shelves/ Bookcases/ Stacking Boxes

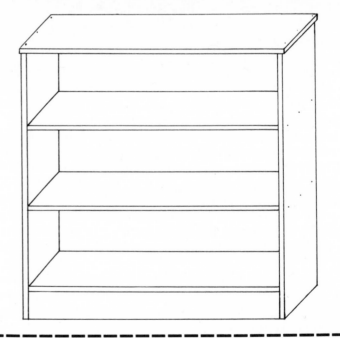

Shelves are shelves are shelves, whether they are for toys or books or clothes . . . with one exception. Toys shelves may become a ladder to an adventuresome child. This means just one more item that must be strong, sturdy, and childproof. Just because it's wonderful to know many variations on building shelves—quickies and slowies—I include variations. However, you must decide which will be the safest. Low shelves don't pose the same danger that high shelves do, and this may be one solution. Later on, as your child is less likely to climb the Matterhorn, you can build floor-to-ceiling shelves.

But shelves you will need! Wait till you see the accumulation of stuffed animals build. We had a zoo! Crocodiles and all. (Now these poor old forgotten animals sit in three large plastic bags up in the attic. My kids don't want them but they won't let me throw them away. Which reminds me . . . I wonder what ever became of *my* teddy?)

Shelves are also useful instead of bureaus. Buy some colored dishpans and use them to store night shirts, panties, gowns, stretch suits, and the like. A few years later when you get around to a bureau, these dishpans can hold the little people, blocks, and all the other little toys that best be separated.

Do not forget the cube and its potential. Stacked cubicle storage. Or, you could revise the cube to a larger size, a rectangle, and add a shelf in the middle.

I have deliberately not suggested standards and brackets because of my own personal disaster. (Standards attach to the wall. Brackets slip into slots on the standards and hold shelves. They either screw into the beams holding the plasterboard, or they can be attached by using molly or toggle bolts that hold the bolt in behind the plaster wall with an expanded-type nut.) In my early novice days, I used mollies that probably didn't go all the way through the plaster and lath and stuff behind.

Yes, my youngest was a mountain climber. Fortunately the shelves were not too high. He climbed one day and the mountain collapsed! Wall, shelves, and thousands of little people and stuffed animals surrounding a rather surprised and miraculously uninjured little boy. So, be advised.

TOY SHELVES/BOOKCASES—PROCEDURE

You may choose from the suggestions the technique that makes you comfortable with the project.

1. From the 1″ x 10″ boards cut one length of 36¼″, two lengths of 35¼″, three lengths of 34¼″.

2. From 2″ x 4″ cut one length of 34½″ and two lengths of 7⅞″.

3. From ¼″ Masonite cut a square panel of 36″ x 36″.

4. Find an old piece of 1″ x 3″ (or buy a new one) 37″ or so to use as a building brace.

5. Measure the sides for the screws and the spacer at bottom and glue and nail them on to the board from inside. Nail the front spacer to the bottom front inside edges of the sides. Predrilling isn't necessary here.

6. Nail the top to the top edges of the sides. Corner-clamp the corners front and back first so it will be squared.

7. Nail the bottom shelf to the front and side spacers.

8. Clamp and screw shelves to sides.

9. Turn the unit on its front edges and nail the Masonite back onto the edge of the sides, top and bottom.

TOY SHELVES/BOOKCASES

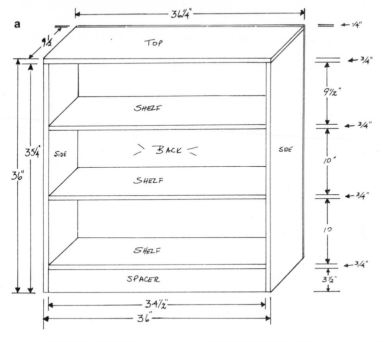

a

36¼"

1½"

TOP

¼"

SHELF

¾"

9½"

35¼" SIDE   > BACK <   SIDE

¾"

36"   SHELF

10"

¾"

SHELF

12"

SPACER

¾"

3½"

34½"

36"

(a) This style is constructed by gluing and screwing shelves to sides.
Build your shelves to your own size needs, but do a drawing like this one to clearly illustrate the lengths of wood for top, sides, and shelves.

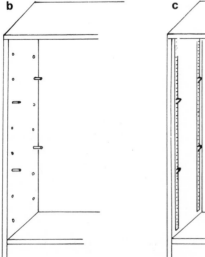

b

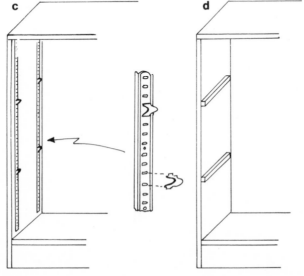

c

d

(b) Movable shelves:
½" diameter holes can be drilled (every 4"–6") in about ½" to receive ½"–⅝" dowel (1½" long) plugs which should be glued. Shelves can sit on dowels.

(c) For movable shelves metal strips and clips can also be used.
Strips screw into sides (¾" flathead screws).

(d) 9" long cleats of ¾" x ¾" may be used for shelf supports; nail them into sides.

TOY SHELVES/BOOKCASES—MATERIALS

1″ x 10″ pine (¾″ x 9½″).　　　　　　　**¼″ Masonite.**

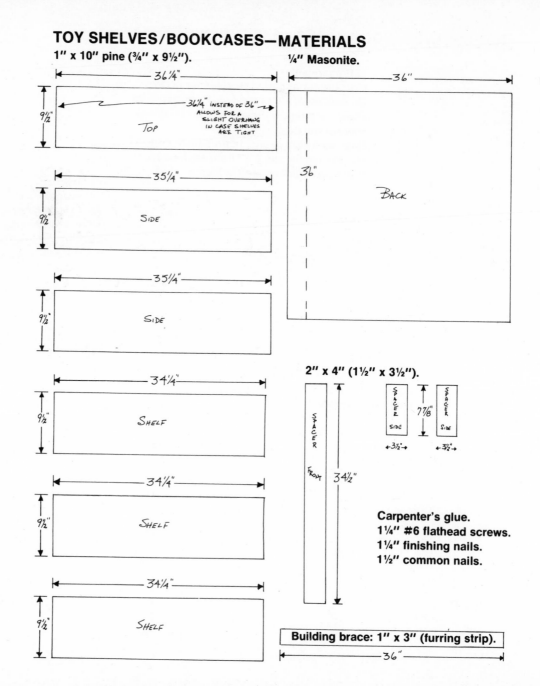

36¼″

9½″

36¼″ INSTEAD OF 36″ ALLOWS FOR A SLIGHT OVERHANG IN CASE SHELVES ARE TIGHT

Top

35¼″

9½″

Side

35¼″

9½″

Side

34¼″

9½″

Shelf

34¼″

9½″

Shelf

34¼″

9½″

Shelf

36″

36″

Back

2″ x 4″ (1½″ x 3½″).

Spacer Front

34½″

Spacer Side

Spacer Side

7⅞″

←3½→　　←3½→

Carpenter's glue.
1¼″ #6 flathead screws.
1¼″ finishing nails.
1½″ common nails.

Building brace: 1″ x 3″ (furring strip).

36″

TOY SHELVES/BOOKCASES—ASSEMBLY

1) Prepare sides:
Measure for and predrill holes for screws:
On outside of side (good side), measure as
shown and lightly draw lines across where
shelves will meet sides.
Next mark drill points, in from each edge 1"
and the center one 4¾" from each edge.
Drill holes from outside to inside.

9½"

¾"

10"

¾"

4¾"

screw
Hole
1"
FROM
edge

center
screw
Hole

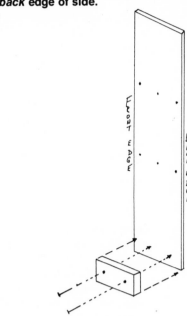

2) Nail side spacers to bottom at sides.
Use 2" common nails. Nail spacer to bottom,
back of each side, making it just flush with
back edge of side.

BACK EDGE

FRONT EDGE

FRONT EDGE

BACK EDGE

**3) Nail left side to left edge of spacer; nail
right side to right edge of front spacer.**
Use 1½" common nails.

MAKE YOUR OWN BABY FURNITURE

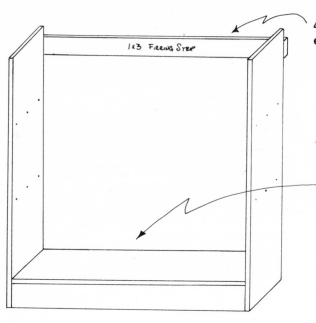

1x3 FURRING STRIP

4) Temporarily nail building brace to back edges of sides to hold structure sturdy.

5) Nail bottom shelf to spacers, side and front.
Use 1½″ common nails.

6) Use corner clamps to hold shelf in position, with shelf edges centered to predrilled holes in sides.
Select a drill bit one size smaller than used for holes inside and drill through side hole into shelf edge about ¼″ in.
Use #6, 1¼″ flathead screws; screw sides to shelf.
Repeat the process for the other shelf.

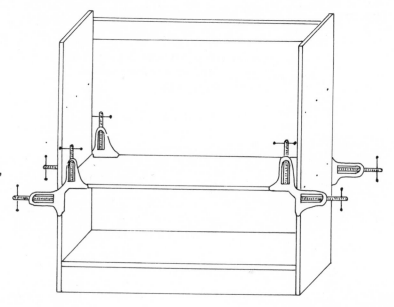

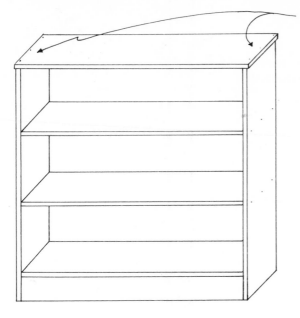

7) Use 1½" finishing nails and nail top to sides.

8) Nail Masonite back to back edges of top and sides.

Use ½" brads.

MAKE YOUR OWN BABY FURNITURE

STACKING BOXES

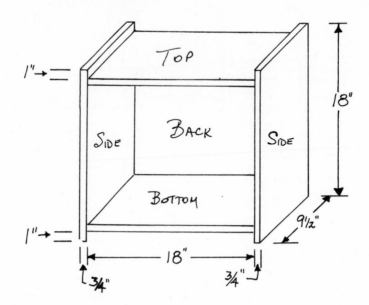

Bang, bang—nail it all together (a little glue, too).

STACKING BOXES—PROCEDURE

For one box:

1. Measure for and cut top, bottom, and sides from a length of 1″ x 10″. Cut the back from a piece of ¼″ Masonite.

2. On the inside of the sides, measure down one inch from top and one inch up from bottom and draw guidelines.

3. Corner-clamp the top and bottom between the sides in front, and nail the front corners together.

4. Corner-clamp the back sections together and then nail the back sections.

5. Midway between front and back nails, hammer a middle nail into the top and bottom from the sides.

6. Turn the unit on its front edges and nail the back on.

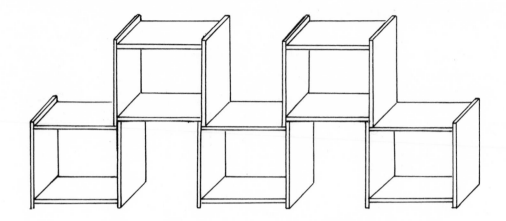

And on . . .
And on . . .

Materials for 1 box 1″ x 10″ (¾″ x 9½″).

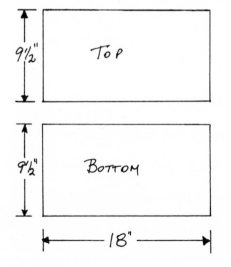

9½″ — TOP — 18″

9½″ — BOTTOM

Mark insides 1″ from edge for setting in top and bottom.

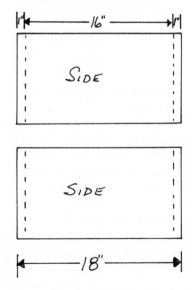

1″ — 16″ — 1″

SIDE

SIDE — 18″

¼″ Masonite.

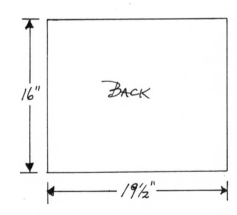

16″ — BACK — 19½″

MAKE YOUR OWN BABY FURNITURE

STACKING BOXES—ASSEMBLY

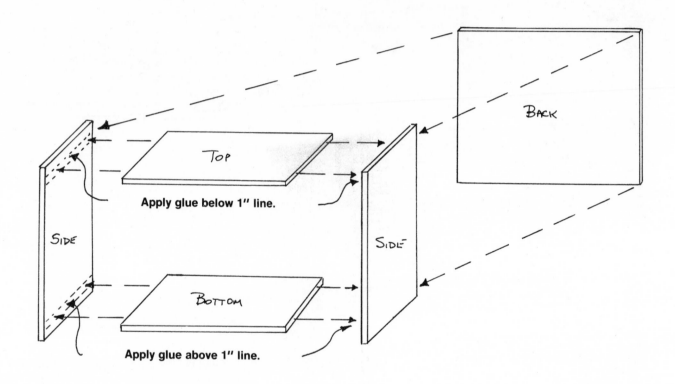

Apply glue below 1" line.

Apply glue above 1" line.

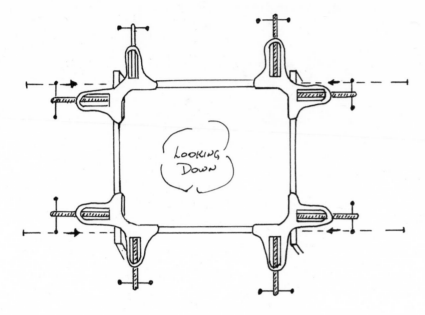

Place sides, top, and bottom on edges, glue, corner-clamp edges, hammer in a 1½" common nail at each corner, about ¾" down. Remove clamps, then box over, repeat above. Midway between the 2 nails on each side hammer another nail in.

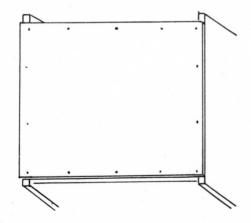

Leaving box on edge, lay the back on, glue and hammer ¾" common nails through the back into the edges of sides, top, and bottom.

Project 12

Tables and Chairs

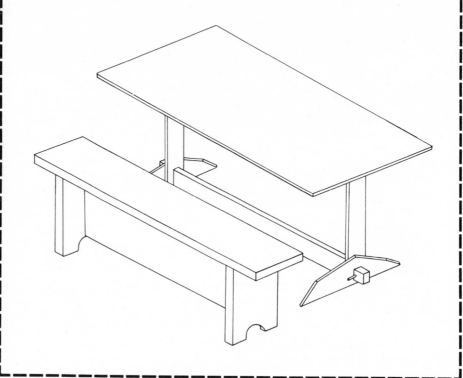

𝒯 wo sets of designs are included. I guess I really favor early American furniture and this is why I include the trestle table as well as the Shaker cradle. As you may have realized by now, all of the plans can be modified for larger or smaller variations. (The Shaker cradle could be a doll cradle. The trestle table could be your dining room table or a desk.)

One of my friends was aesthetically disturbed that the bench for the trestle table was of thick wood and the table itself was thinner wood. It's easier to make a sturdy bench that way. That's how I feel—and I suspect that the bench will be turned on its side to be used in other kinds of play. I'm not really bothered by things that don't match so much as I am by things that don't function.

I would like to make a suggestion about the tables. It might be a good idea to edge the table with 1¼"-wide lath, so the lath sits with the width higher than the table top. This will keep pieces of puzzles and games and food from falling off when the child is young. Later it can be removed. Just glue it and hammer in some finishing nails to hold it on.

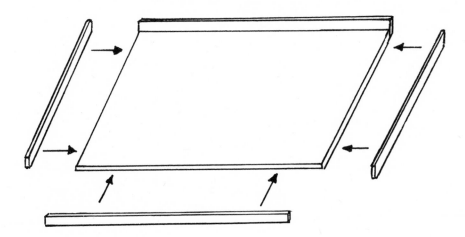

TABLE AND CHAIRS FOR TODDLER

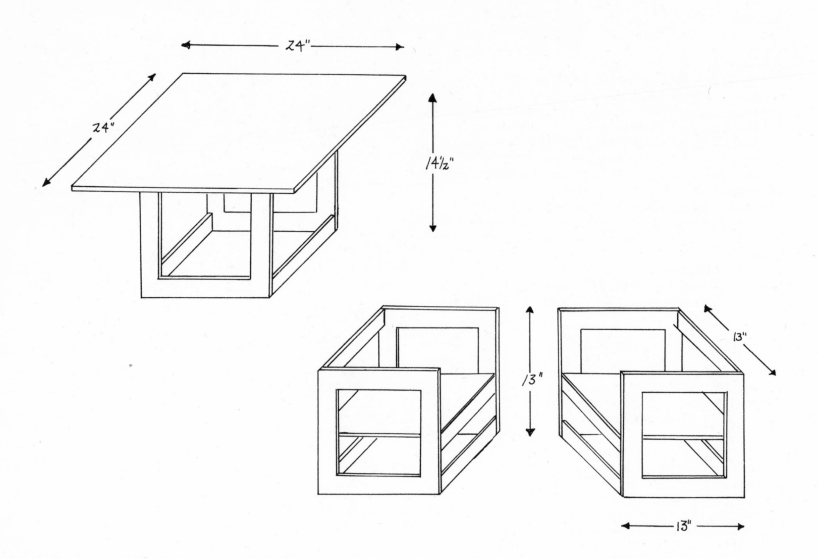

TODDLER TABLE AND CHAIRS—PROCEDURE

½″ Plywood

1. Measure for the first cut, 25″ into the 48″ side, then measure for the second cut, the other side of the table top, 24″. Make the first, then second cut, yielding the table top.

2. Measure for the third cut, 25″ into the 48″ side, and cut it.
Measure for the fourth cut of 25″, and cut it.
Measure for the fifth cut, and cut it, yielding two chair sides.
Measure for the sixth cut, and cut it, yielding two chair seats.

3. Measure for the seventh cut, and cut it.
Measure for the eighth cut, and cut it.
Measure for the ninth cut, and cut it, yielding two table sides.

4. Measure for the tenth cut, and cut it.
Measure for the eleventh cut, and cut it.
Measure for the twelfth cut, and cut it, yielding two chair sides.

5. From the 1″ x 2″ measure for and cut, one at a time, four lengths of 13″ and ten lengths of 12″.

6. Measure for the cut-out squares in the table sides and chair sides, and cut them out. Start by drilling a hole big enough for the saw blade to enter.

7. Sand all the pieces well.

Table

8. Measure for the top iron angle braces, in an inch from the corners, and screw them in. No predrilling for these screws, usually thin, is required. The plywood will hold them.

9. Corner-clamp the table base pieces together, predrill, and screw the table sides to the 1″ x 3″ spacers. Do front first, then back, if you have only four corner clamps.

10. Measure the under side of the table top for its placement on the base; draw guide lines.

11. Lay the table top, underside up, on the floor. Apply glue to the inner borders of where the base will sit. Turn the base upside down and lay it on the table top within the guide lines. Screw the angles of the base into the table top.

MAKE YOUR OWN BABY FURNITURE

Chair

12. Measure for the placement of the seat braces on the sides.

13. Corner-clamp the back upper and lower braces to the sides, predrill, and screw together.

14. Corner-clamp the back seat brace to the sides, predrill, and screw together.

15. Corner-clamp the front lower brace and the front seat brace to the sides, predrill, and screw together.

16. Apply glue to the upper edges of the seat braces and lay the seat in the braces. A few finishing nails from seat to brace will add security.

TABLE AND CHAIRS FOR TODDLER—MATERIALS

Pine: 1″ x 2″ (¾″ x 1¾″).

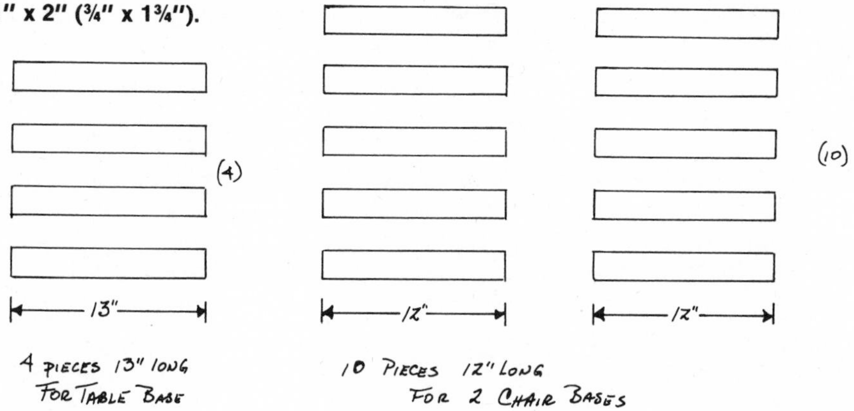

(4)

|← 13″ →|

4 pieces 13″ long
for Table Base

(10)

|← 12″ →| |← 12″ →|

10 pieces 12″ long
for 2 Chair Bases

Angle Braces: (6)
2 for table base
4 for attaching table top to base.

1¼″ #6 screws and carpenter's glue.

½" plywood (A-D).

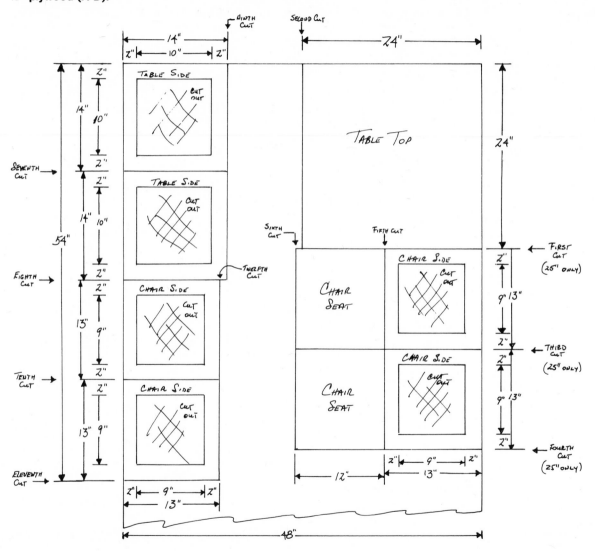

TABLE AND CHAIRS FOR TODDLER—ASSEMBLY

Detail: Attach angles to sides allowing space for 1″ x 3″ cross-piece.
After base pieces are joined, turn over onto table top under side and attach angles to top.

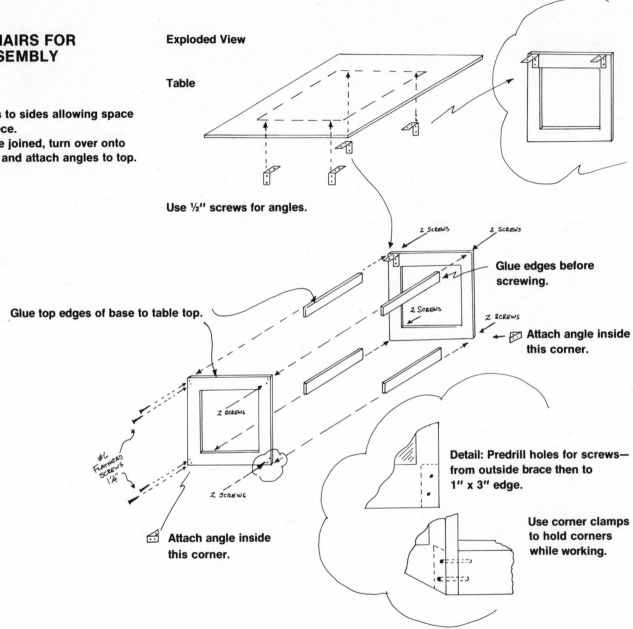

Exploded View

Table

Use ½″ screws for angles.

Z screws   Z screws

Glue edges before screwing.

Z Screws

Z screws

Glue top edges of base to table top.

Attach angle inside this corner.

Z screws

#L FLATHEAD SCREWS 1'4"

Z SCREWS

Attach angle inside this corner.

Detail: Predrill holes for screws— from outside brace then to 1″ x 3″ edge.

Use corner clamps to hold corners while working.

TABLE AND CHAIRS FOR TODDLER—ASSEMBLY

Exploded view

Chair.

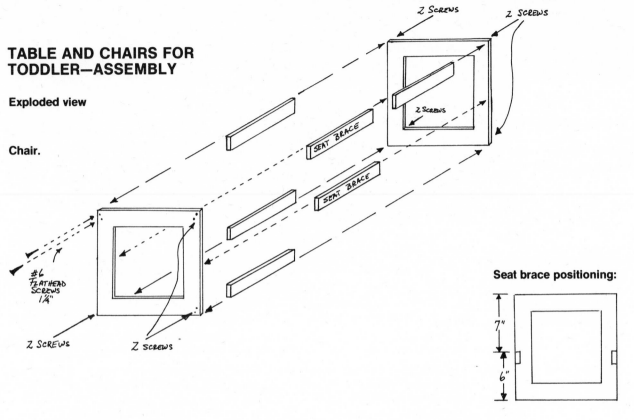

2 SCREWS

2 SCREWS

2 SCREWS

SEAT BRACE

SEAT BRACE

#6 FLATHEAD SCREWS 1¼"

2 SCREWS

2 SCREWS

Seat brace positioning:

7"

6"

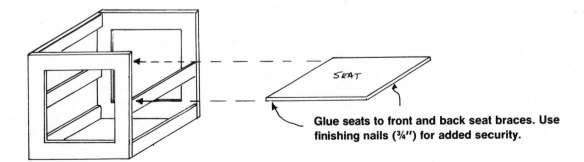

SEAT

Glue seats to front and back seat braces. Use finishing nails (¾") for added security.

TRESTLE TABLE AND BENCH—PROCEDURE

For the table

1. Measure for and cut the table top from a piece of ¾″ or ½″ plywood.

2. From 2″ x 4″ measure for and cut two lengths of 34″.

3. From 1″ x 6″ measure for and cut four lengths of 18″.

4. From 1″ x 4″ measure for and cut two lengths of 18″.

5. From ¾″-diameter dowel measure for and cut four lengths of 4″.

For the bench

6. From 2″ x 8″ measure for and cut two lengths of 10½″, one length of 36″ and one length of 29″.

Table

7. Using the pattern included, measure for the cleat cut on each leg cleat of 1″ x 6″. Measure for the mortise cut-out, predrill a hole for the saw blade to fit, and cut out the mortise. Then cut out the shape of the cleat on each piece.

8. Measure for the mortise cuts on the leg posts (1″ x 4″), predrill a hole for the saw blade, and cut out the mortise holes.

9. Measure for the tenon cutoffs on the 2″ x 4″ cross-pieces. Saw ¾″ in on each end and chisel the wood off. (See "Construction Techniques" for doing this sort of thing.)

10. Measure for and drill holes in the cross-pieces for the dowel plugs.

11. Glue and screw the legs to the cleats as shown.

12. Slip the tenon ends of the cross-pieces through the mortises of the cleated table legs and peg together.

13. Measure the underside of the table top for its placement on the base.

14. Screw angle to the legs near the outer upper edges.

15. Lay the table top on the floor, underside up, and glue the inner borders of the base guidelines.

16. Lay the base upside down on the table top and screw the base angles into the table top.

Bench

17. Measure for the placement of the cross-piece between the two leg pieces.

18. Corner-clamp the cross-piece between the legs and nail the legs to the cross-piece.

19. Glue all the top edges of the base and lay the seat on top. Nail the seat to the base.

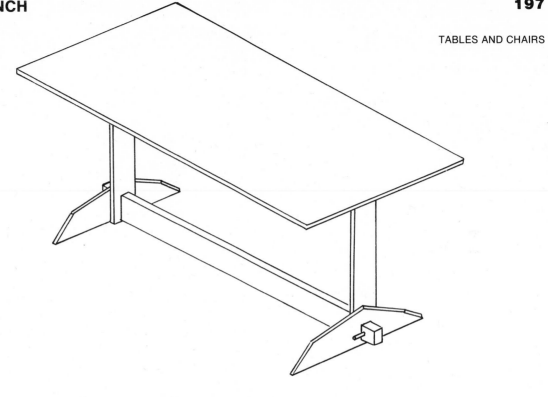

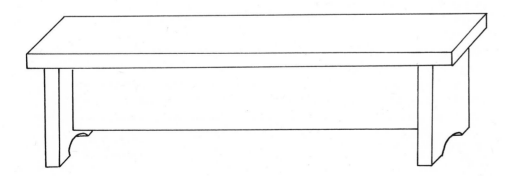

TRESTLE TABLE—MATERIALS

Table top: plywood ¾″ or ½″ (A-D).

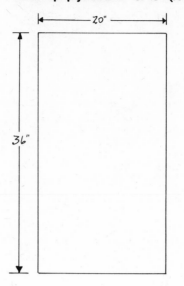

Cleats (4) for leg: 1″ x 6″ pine (¾″ x 5½″).

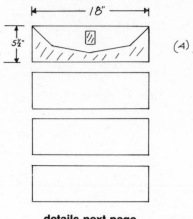

(4)

details next page

Note: **Total length is 6′. It is necessary to buy a length of 1″ x 6″ longer than 6′ because some wood will be lost in sawing off pieces.**

Cross-pieces (2): 2″ x 4″ (1½″ x 3½″).

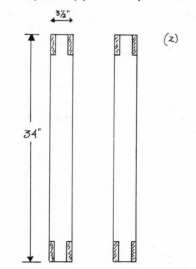

(2)

Leg posts (2) 1″ x 4″ pine (¾″ x 3½″).

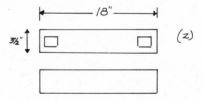

(2)

Cross-piece pegs (4): ¾″ dowel 3″ or 4″ long.

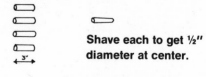

Shave each to get ½″ diameter at center.

**Screws (16) #8 flathead 1¼″ long.
Carpenter's glue.**

(16) ½″ screws for angles.

Angles (4) 2″ by 1″

TRESTLE TABLE—DETAILS

Cleats for legs (1″ x 6″).

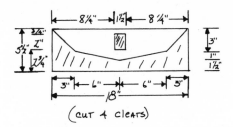

(CUT 4 CLEATS)

Leg posts (1″ x 4″).

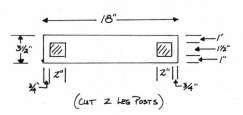

(CUT 2 LEG POSTS)

Cross-pieces: (2″ x 4″).

TENON

1) Do before chiseling:

Use chisel along line to break off piece.

SAW THROUGH ¾″

Saw through ¾″.

Mark dot and puncture with awl—for drilling ½″ hole for peg.

MAKE YOUR OWN BABY FURNITURE

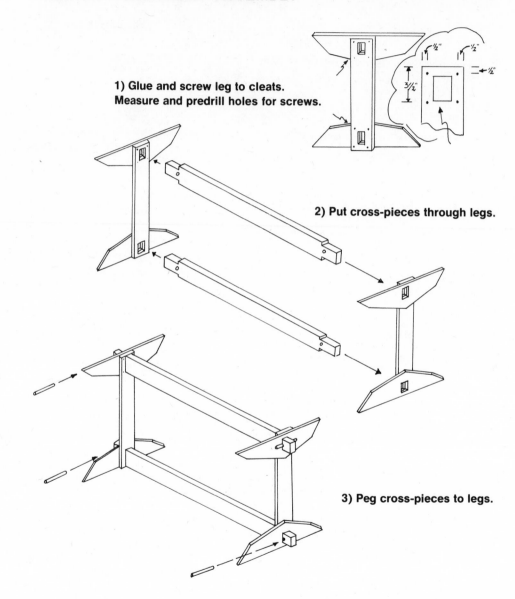

1) Glue and screw leg to cleats.
Measure and predrill holes for screws.

2) Put cross-pieces through legs.

3) Peg cross-pieces to legs.

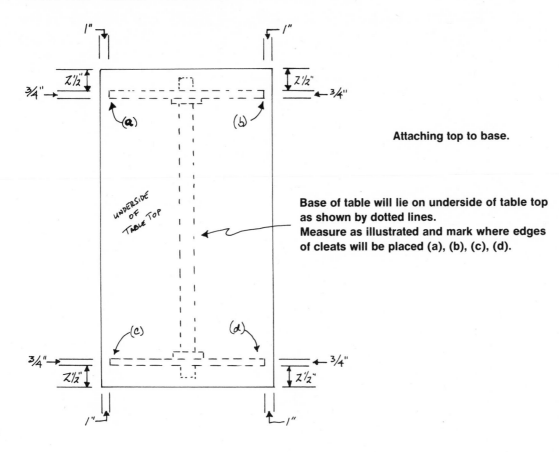

Attaching top to base.

Base of table will lie on underside of table top as shown by dotted lines.
Measure as illustrated and mark where edges of cleats will be placed (a), (b), (c), (d).

Glue top of base to under side of table top (weight while glue dries, about 1 hour).
Attach cleats to table top with angles (use 1″ x 2″ angles and ½″ screws).

BENCH FOR TRESTLE TABLE—MATERIALS

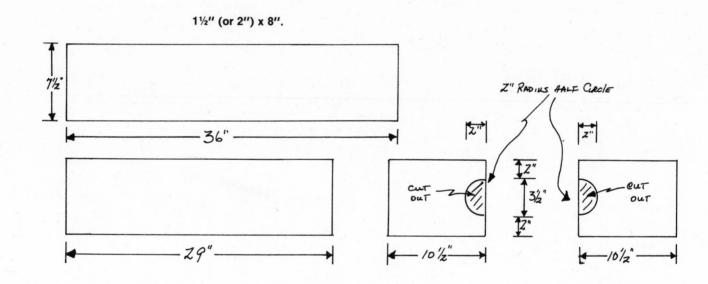

1½″ (or 2″) x 8″.

7½″

36″

29″

2″ RADIUS HALF CIRCLE

2″

2″

CUT OUT

2″

3½″

2″

CUT OUT

10½″

10½″

BENCH FOR TRESTLE TABLE—ASSEMBLY

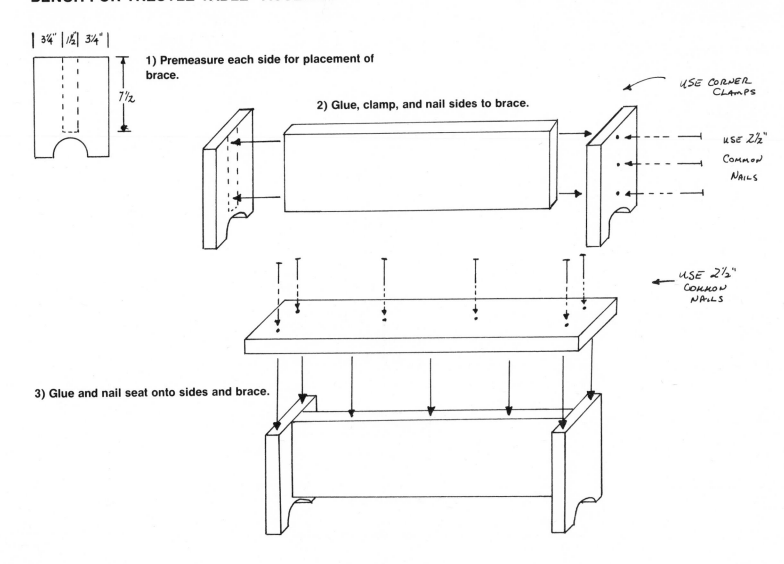

3¼" | 1½ | 3¼"

7½

1) Premeasure each side for placement of brace.

2) Glue, clamp, and nail sides to brace.

USE CORNER CLAMPS

USE 2½" COMMON NAILS

USE 2½" COMMON NAILS

3) Glue and nail seat onto sides and brace.

Project 13

MOMMY ROCKER

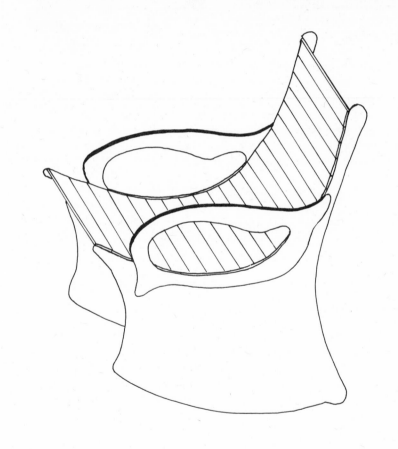

I had a wonderful thrift-shop rocker that was a perfect fit for me. I nursed both boys while sitting in it. And I hummed and sang baby-kind soft, gentle songs to them while I rocked slowly. The rocker was, in fact, my pacifier, particularly at the 5 AM feeding, when I needed something to distract me from my selfish mood of "Damn it, I want to be in bed!" That may sound like mommy-treason, and well it may be, but it also represents an honesty you may come to know, almost surely.

Maybe the significance of a rocker is its ancient history. Coming to us from ages ago in BC, it brings the same purpose it has always had—a place for mommy and baby. In the early days of America, when pioneer wagons traveled across the country, there was often a collapsible rocker tucked in the wagon for a mother traveling with her baby.

Yes, a kind of magic spell, a peaceable kingdom, yes, this may be what a rocker is.

You may want to build your own rocker. However, this may be the one piece of "baby furniture" you would enjoy antique hunting for. I have found three completely different and yet comfortable rockers in the past few years, each quite inexpensive and each durable, though old. Think on that awhile, before you plunge in to build the rocker described here.

The rocker for mommy is fairly easy to assemble. Two shapes are cut from plywood, the ends sanded, and back and front and inner braces are attached. A few dozen wooden slats are nailed to the upper edges of the sides. The armrests are then attached. You could also add some box-pockets on the sides.

The whole thing should then be sanded completely. The rocker may then be polyurethaned or painted, your choice.

Since this is to be your own creation, you can make any modification you wish. Often I am hesitant to alter a store-bought item, but if it is something I made myself I have no pause. A custom made mommy-toy, I guess, is what this rocker can become.

MAKE YOUR OWN BABY FURNITURE

MOMMY ROCKER

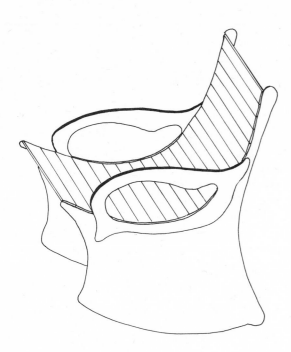

MOMMY ROCKER—PROCEDURE

1. Make an actual-size template for the side and the armrest. Trace them onto the ¾" plywood twice, as shown. Puncture holes through the template to the plywood for the screw holes for the spacers and armrests. Cut out the pieces.

2. From the 2" x 2" measure for and cut six lengths of 22½".

3. From the hardwood lattice measure for and cut 30 lengths of 24".

4. Predrill through the plywood for the spacers, but not for armrests. Predrill screw holes in armrests.

5. Get some help—to hold the spacers—and nail through the holes in the plywood into the spacers on one side, then do the other side. On the second side do not hammer the nails all the way through.

6. Turn the unit onto the side where the nails are all the way in. On the side where the nails are only partially driven in, carefully, holding a spacer in position, remove the nail for that spacer and drill through the plywood into the spacer. Screw side to spacer. Then go on to the next spacer and repeat, until all the spacers on one side are finished.

7. Turn the unit over onto the other side. Hammer up from inside the side near all the spacers. Then hammer down from the outside of the side. The nails should now be sticking out so they can be removed. (If this doesn't work for you, hammer the side completely off, remove the nails and then hammer them partially in again.) Then repeat step 6 for this side; screw the side to the spacers.

8. ⅜" in from each end of each length of lattice, predrill a very thin hole, about one-half to three-quarters the diameter of the nail.

9. Starting at the seat end, rather than the head end, of the chair, glue the upper edges of the sides and lay the lattice lengths on, nailing each in position as it is laid.

10. After the seat area is covered, lay the chair on its back, with some bracing under the head end, so that it lies almost flat, and continue gluing and nailing the lattice on until finished.

11. Partially nail the armrests in position and, removing one nail at a time, screw it into the side. No predrilling in the side is necessary, for the plywood won't split from these screws.

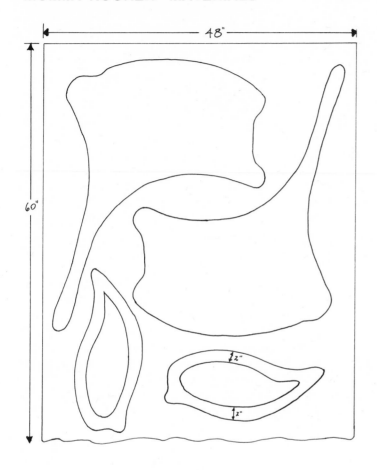

48"

60"

¾" plywood (A-D).

See templates next page.

2" x 2" (1½" x 1½") for spacers (6).

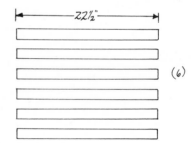

22½"

(6)

1" x 2" (¾" x 1½") finished hardwood strips.

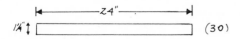

24"

¼"

(30)

Carpenter's glue.
1½" #8 flathead screws.
1¼" finishing nails.

MAKE YOUR OWN BABY FURNITURE

(a) Screw hole for armrest.
(s) Screw hole for spacer.

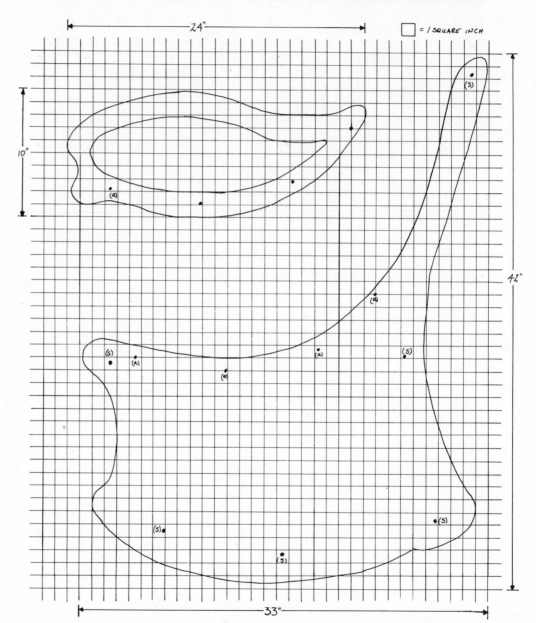

Screw sides to spacers.

Use 1½″ #8 flathead screws.

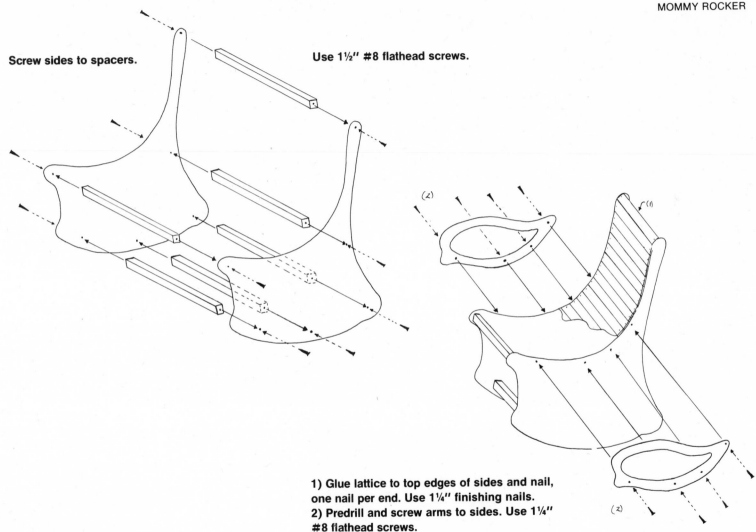

1) Glue lattice to top edges of sides and nail, one nail per end. Use 1¼″ finishing nails.
2) Predrill and screw arms to sides. Use 1¼″ #8 flathead screws.

210

Project 14

BUILT-IN: CRIB/ CHANGING TABLE/ BUREAU/ YOUTH BED

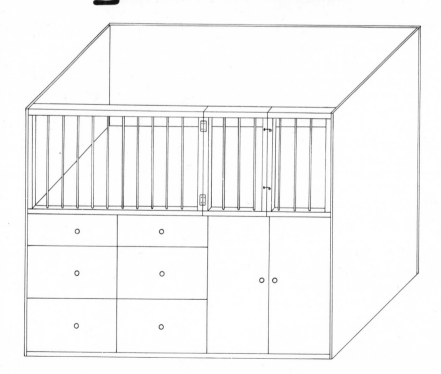

There is much to be said in favor of the "built-in." My favorite reason being that you don't have to clean underneath . . . no furniture to move . . . that sort of thing. A built-in of the design I am about to offer will also save space. And it is a piece which grows without growing. Space under cribs and beds is usually always wasted empty space. This needn't be.

Whether or not you can go the built-in route may be determined by your room layout . . . where windows and doors are, that sort of limit. If you can do it, however, the benefits will be obvious, particularly because you can build this right at the beginning, while the baby is still in the cradle, carriage, drawer, or box.

You have already seen the ideas for the crib and changing table, where the changing table can later become a bureau. Why not incorporate these into one, since the baby is either in the crib or on the changing table. So let the crib also be used as the changing table. And if we elongate the crib, it may later be a youth bed, with only half-sides. Finally, when your child has outgrown the youth bed, the half-sides can be removed and it becomes a bed. A bed for all seasons. Neat.

The crib side will be partially a gate which opens to remove the baby, and while open the crib can be the changing table. Later the gate can be removed. The bed's height is up to you. I suggest a table height, for ease of lifting the bigger baby out. Beneath will be shelves, with or without doors, or drawers—your choice. I have also included a simple ladder to be added when the child is old enough to get out of bed herself.

It's kind of like building a whole environment for your baby as soon as she's born.

The bonus of this plan is that there is no furniture to dispose of and replace. At this time, when inflation is dogging us so badly, it seems very wise to invest in permanent fixtures. Further, in the end you will discover that the cost of buying all the wood to build this structure will be less than the cost of a sturdy crib and bureau.

MAKE YOUR OWN BABY FURNITURE

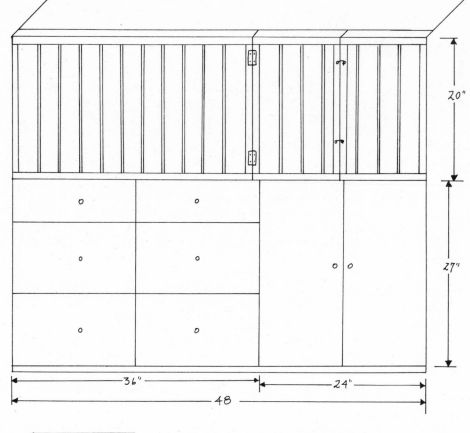

This is actually your project to design and work out—built-ins usually are fit into wall niches. Your dimensions. Follow the crib instructions for the doweling. I have included guiding dimensions.

Doors can be removed when child is old enough for youth bed.
Opens to pick baby up, can be changing place.

Hanging closet or shelf closet or open shelves.

The frame must be ¾" plywood for strength.

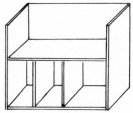

Ladder: 2" x 4" with ⅝" dowels, 10" long, through it (glued and finishing nailed).

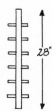

Appendix

SAWHORSES

Make from scrap lumber; make 2.

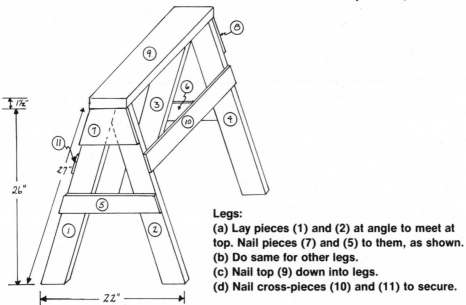

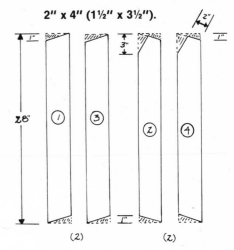

2" x 4" (1½" x 3½").

(2) (2)

1" x 3" (¾" x 2½").

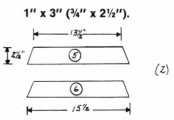

(2)

Legs:
(a) Lay pieces (1) and (2) at angle to meet at top. Nail pieces (7) and (5) to them, as shown.
(b) Do same for other legs.
(c) Nail top (9) down into legs.
(d) Nail cross-pieces (10) and (11) to secure.

1" x 6" (¾" x 5½").

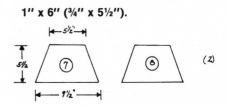

(2)

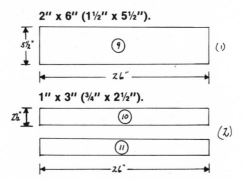

2" x 6" (1½" x 5½").

(1)

1" x 3" (¾" x 2½").

(2)

HOW TO DRAW AN OVAL, GIVEN HEIGHT AND WIDTH

Given that we want an oval 4″ by 6″:
1) Draw lines AB (6″) and CD (4″), crossing at center point E;
2) Construct a ruler where the distance from arrow (1) to arrow (2) = length CE (2″) and the distance from arrow (1) to arrow (3) = length AE (3″).
(You could paste little pieces of paper on a ruler.)

For large ovals just draw 1 quadrant and trace it for other 3.

Moving the ruler around in such a way that arrow (3) is touching line CD while arrow (2) is touching line AB at the same time will give the X points at arrow (1).

A wonderful gadget for helping form curves is this "French Curve."

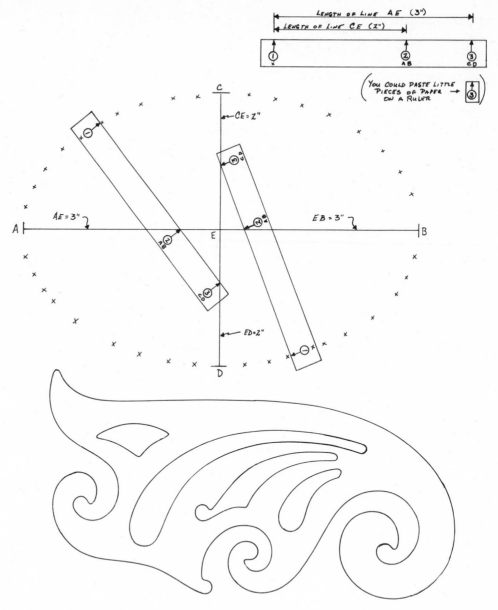

LENGTH OF LINE AE (3")

LENGTH OF LINE CE (2")

(YOU COULD PASTE LITTLE PIECES OF PAPER ON A RULER)

C

CE = 2"

A ⊢ AE = 3" E EB = 3" B

ED = 2"

D

LUMBER PRICE GUIDE

Strips and Boards:

Name	Actual Size	Price, Dec. 1978	*Check with your lumber yard and fill in the prices so you can anticipate the cost of each project*
parting bead	3/8″ x 3/4″	14¢/ft.	_____
baluster	1-1/16″ x 1-1/16″	50¢/ft.	_____
lattice	1/4″ x 1-5/16″	15¢/ft.	_____
1″ x 1″	3/4″ x 3/4″	30¢/ft.	_____
1″ x 2″	3/4″ x 1½″	27¢/ft.	_____
1″ x 3″	3/4″ x 2½″	45¢/ft.	_____
firring strip	3/4″ x 2½″ (rough)	8¢/ft.	_____
1″ x 4″	3/4″ x 3½″	29¢/ft.	_____
1″ x 6″	3/4″ x 5½″	45¢/ft.	_____
1″ x 8″	3/4″ x 7½″	61¢/ft.	_____
1″ x 10″	3/4″ x 9½″	74¢/ft.	_____
1″ x 12″	3/4″ x 11½″	89¢/ft.	_____
1″ x 8″, wide	5/4″ x 7½″	83¢/ft.	_____
1″ x 14″, wide	5/4″ x 13½″	1.46/ft.	_____
2″ x 2″	1½″ x 1½″	35¢/ft.	_____
2″ x 3″	1½″ x 2½″	30¢/ft.	_____
2″ x 4″	1½″ x 3½″	25¢/ft.	_____

Panels:

1/4″-thick plywood (A-C)	4′ x 8′	$14.00	_____
1/2″-thick plywood (A-C)	4′ x 8′	17.60	_____
3/4″-thick plywood (A-C)	4′ x 8′	23.68	_____
3/16″-thick Masonite	4′ x 4′	3.36	_____
1/4″-thick Masonite	4′ x 8′	7.83	_____

Dowels:

1/4″ diameter	4′ length	40¢/each	_____
3/8″ diameter	4′ length	45¢/each	_____
1/2″ diameter	4′ length	49¢/each	_____
5/8″ diameter	4′ length	56¢/each	_____
3/4″ diameter	4′ length	63¢/each	_____
1″ diameter	4′ length	89¢/each	_____
1¼″ diameter		37¢/ft.	_____
1⅜″ (closet pole)		42¢/ft.	_____

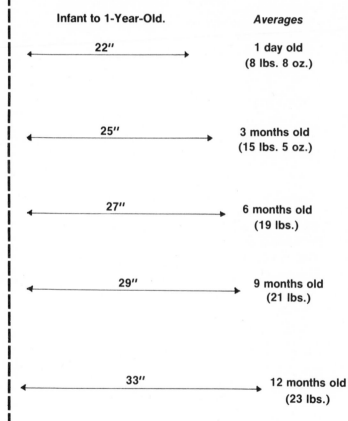

AVERAGE BABY SIZES

Infant to 1-Year-Old.   *Averages*

22″   **1 day old**
(8 lbs. 8 oz.)

25″   **3 months old**
(15 lbs. 5 oz.)

27″   **6 months old**
(19 lbs.)

29″   **9 months old**
(21 lbs.)

33″   **12 months old**
(23 lbs.)

SHOPPING LISTS

Material	Size/Length	Quantity	Supplies
CRADLE/TOYBOX/ROCKING CHAIR			
¾" plywood (A-D)	4' x 8'	1	Carpenter's glue
Offset hinges (¾" offset)	2" long	2	1¼" #8 flathead screws
			1½" #8 flathead screws
SHAKER CRADLE			
¾" plywood (A-D)	4' x 51"	1	Carpenter's glue
1" x 6" (¾" x 5½") pine	4'	1	1¼" #8 flathead screws
1" x 1" (true) or baluster			
(1-1/16" x 1-1/16")	27"	1	
⅜"-diameter dowel	6"	1	
CHANGING TABLE			
½" plywood (A-D)	4' x 8'	2	Carpenter's glue
2" x 4" (1½" x 3½")	8½'	1	¾" brads
Parting bead (⅜" x ¾")	10'	2	1" #6 flathead screws
Parting bead (⅜" x ¾")	12'	1	1½" common nails
			2½" common nails
BOX FOR TOP			
Leftover ½" plywood			1" brads, glue
DOORS OPTION			
Leftover ½" plywood	34¾" x 31⅜"	1	Screws—½" should
			come with hinges.
Offset hinges (½" offset)	2" long	4	
DRAWERS OPTION			
½" plywood (A-D)	4' x 8'	1	Carpenters glue
Drawer knobs	—	6	1" #6 flathead screws
and some leftover plywood	(13')	(3)	(1¼" #8 flathead
(or 1" x 10" pine boards)			screws)
BABY SEAT			
¼" or ½" plywood (A-D)	6⅓' x 11½"	1	1" #6 flathead screws
or 1" x 12" pine pieces			1¼" #6 flathead screws
1" x 3" (¾" x 2½")	44"	1	¼" screws
½"-diameter dowel	42"	1	
1¼"-diameter dowel	9"	1	
half-circle braces	⅜" radius	2	
butt hinges	½" x 2"	2	
Padded material			

Material	Size/Length	Quantity	Supplies
CRIB/DESK			
½" plywood (A-D)	4' x 8'	2	Carpenter's glue
2" x 4" (1½" x 3½")	14' (cut 9½',	1	1¼" #6 flathead screws
	4¼' to carry)		2½" common nails
Baluster (1-1/16" x 1-1/16")	10'	2	
Baluster (1-1/16" x 1-1/16")	6'	1	
⅝"-diameter dowel	4'	13	
Butt hinges			
(permanent pins)	½" x 2"	3	
⅝"-diameter bolts	3"	4	
with nuts	for ⅝"	4	
and washers	for ⅝"	8	
HIGH CHAIR			
1" x 12" (¾" x 11½")	9'	1	Carpenter's glue
½" plywood (A-D)	49½" x 19½"	1	1¼" #8 flathead screws
1" x 3" (¾" x 2½")	26"	1	
Baluster (1-1/16" x 1-1/16")	8'	1	
⅜"-diameter bolts	1½"	2	
with nuts	for ⅜"	2	
and washers	for ⅜"	4	
Butt hinges	½" x 2"	2	
Hook and eye (with safety)	2"	1	
PLAYPEN/PLAYHOUSE			
Baluster (1-1/16" x 1-1/16")	8'	9	Carpenter's glue
4: 42⅛" + 42⅛"			¾" #6 flathead screws
4: 42⅛" + 42⅛"			1" #6 flathead screws
4: 24"			1½" #8 flathead screws
4: 24"			2" #8 flathead screws
4: 24"			
2: 24", 1: 36"			
4: 20", 1: 15"			
4: 20", 1: 15"			
1: 36", 2: 15"			
⅝"-diameter dowel	24¾"	10	
(if one side doweled)			
Butt hinges	1" x 2"	12	
Butt hinges	1" x 3"	4	
⅜" Masonite—playpen:	4' x 8'	1	
	4' x 4'	1	
extra for playhouse:	4' x 8'	1	
	4' x 4'	1	

Material	Size/Length	Quantity	Supplies
SWING			
1½''-diameter dowel	4'	1	
⅝''-diameter dowel	4'	3	
Cotter pins	1¼''	32	
½'' rope	20'		
Canvas	1 yd, 2'' w.		
SWING FRAME			
2'' x 4'' (1½'' x 3½'')	12'	3	1½'' #8 flathead screws
	7'	1	
1'' x 8'' (¾'' x 7½'')	9'	1	
	6'	1	
½''-diameter bolts	2''	10	
with nuts	for ½'' bolts	10	
and washers	for ½'' bolts	20	
WALKER			
¾'' plywood (A-D)	28'' x 28''	1	Staple gun
⅜''-diameter threaded rods	12''	4	
with nuts	for ⅜''	8	
and lock washers	for ⅜''	8	
and washers	for ⅜''	8	
and cap nuts	for ⅜''	4	
Wheels	—	4	
Material for seat	14'' x 24''		
(strong canvas)			
ROCKER/VEHICLE			
½'' plywood (A-D)	22'' x 23''	1	Carpenter's glue
1'' x 12'' (¾'' x 11½'')	4'	1	1¼'' common nails
2'' x 4'' (1½'' x 3½'')	26''	1	1'' #6 flathead screws
1'' x 1'' (true)	13''	1	
ROCKER/VEHICLE SIDES			
½'' plywood (A-D)	varies		
e.g., elephant	21'' x 34''	2	
Wheels for vehicle	—	4	

Material	Size/Length	Quantity	Supplies
SEESAW			
1'' x 6'' (¾'' x 5½'')	5'	1	Carpenter's glue
1'' x 12'' (¾'' x 11½'')	20''	1	½'' flathead screws
1'' x 8'' (¾'' x 7½'')	21½''	1	1¼'' #8 flathead screws
2'' x 4'' (1½'' x 3½'')	1'	1	
1¼''-diameter dowel	10''	1	
¾''-diameter dowel	16''	1	
Cotter pins	2''	2	
half-circle braces	1¼'' radius	2	
BUILDING BLOCKS			
2'' x 4'' (1½'' x 3½'')	as much		
2''-diameter dowel	as you		
¼'' x ¾'' lattice	want		
PEOPLE/ENVIRONMENTS			
1¼''-diameter dowel	3''/person		
scrap leftovers			
(for environments)			
GADGET BOARD			
(From scraps)			
¼'' plywood (A-D)	3¼'' x 3¼''	5	
2'' x 4'' (1½'' x 3½'')	2½'' x ¾''	1	
⅜''-diameter dowel	6''	1	
Piece of plastic			
(milk container)	2½'' x ½''	1	
Cotter pins	¾''	8	
PUZZLES			
¼'' plywood (A-D) (shapes)	4' x 16''	1 (8 puzzles)	
⅛'' Masonite (backing)	4' x 16''	1 (8 puzzles)	
PUZZLE SHELVES			
½'' plywood (A-D)	4' x 10½''	1	Carpenter's glue
Parting bead (½'' x ⅜'')	12½'	1	¾'' brads (thin)
			¾'' common nails

MAKE YOUR OWN BABY FURNITURE

SHOPPING LISTS

Material	Size/Length	Quantity	Supplies
EASEL			
½″ plywood or Masonite	18″ x 18″	3	
Butt hinges	½″ x 2″	4	
Binder clips	large	2	
Hook and eye	2″	2	
TOYSHELVES/BOOKCASE			
1″ x 10″ (¾″ x 9½″)	12′	1	Carpenter's glue
1″ x 10″ (¾″ x 9½″)	6′	1	1¼″ #6 flathead screws
2″ x 4″ (1½″ x 3½″)	41½″	1	1¼″ finishing nails
¼″ Masonite	3′ x 3′	1	1½″ common nails
1″ x 3″ (furring: ¾″ x 2½″)	3′	1	½″ brads
STACKING SHELVES			
1″ x 10″ (¾″ x 9½″) (1 box)	6′	1	Carpenter's glue
¼″ Masonite (1 box)	16″ x 19½″	1	¾″ common nails
			1½″ common nails

Material	Size/Length	Quantity	Supplies
TODDLER TABLE AND CHAIRS			
½″ plywood (A-D)	4′ x 54″	1	Carpenter's glue
1″ x 2″ (¾″ x 1½″)	16′	1	1¼″ #8 flathead screws
Angle braces	½″ x 2″	6	¾″ finishing nails
TRESTLE TABLE AND BENCH			
½″ or ¾″ plywood (A-D)	36″ x 20″	1	Carpenter's glue
2″ x 4″ (1½″ x 3½″)	68″	1	1¼″ #8 flathead screws
1″ x 6″ (¾″ x 5½″)	6′	1	2½″ common nails
1″ x 4″ (¾″ x 3½″)	3′	1	
¾″-diameter dowel	1′	1	
Angle irons	1″ x 2″	4	
1½″ or 2″ x 8″ or 8½″	7′2″	1	
MOMMY ROCKER			
¾″ plywood (A-D)	4′ x 60″	1	Carpenter's glue
2″ x 2″ (1½″ x 1½″)	12′	1	1½″ #8 flathead screws
¾″ x lattice, *hardwood*	12′	5	1¼″ finishing nails